Descendants of Sarah Watson

Compiled by Leonard
Hendershott
September 13, 2020

Compiled by Leonard

Foreword

I create these books using Family Book Creator, a plug-in for Family Tree Maker (FTM). I enter my information on Ancestry.com and synchronize this data to FTM. I then utilize FTM to perform maintenance operations on the dataset including *place name resolving* (describing place names by [country], [state/province/parish], [county], [township/city], [postal address] - up to five identifiers ordered by most specific to most general) which permits the listing of my subjects by location. FTM also has a wide variety of other genealogical report formats which can be accessed to enhance publications. I publish separate nodes as I complete a branch of my family tree (now over 30,000 subjects) and publish them using Lulu Publishing.

This book contains the facts, who, where, when, but not the story of the descendants of Sarah Jane Watson (1853-1931), my 3rd great aunt. If you can add to our history or have an anecdote to tell, then please share it and help make our story come alive. Even little things, like your cousin the fisherman who didn't eat fish, will make our story more personal. If you can add to our story, please contact me! I hope to have at least a photo of everyone who is here. It is amazing how often there is a close resemblance for relatives separated by generations.

Leonard
Hendershott
September 13, 2020

Contents

Introduction

The following pages list data for all known family members as of September 13, 2020.

Each immediate family is presented in their own section that contains a graphical family tree as well as a description with information about each referenced person and their children. The child section provides information about the children of the preceding couple. When a child has offspring of their own this is presented in a separate family section for that child. In this case a '+' is used to denote that an individual will appear later in the book as a parent with his/her own children and there is a link to the appropriate family reference number. For children with partners but no offspring the partner data is given with the reference family. Roman numerals, followed by a period, are used to indicate the birth order.

In the chapter titled "Family of the Starting Person" the ancestors of Sarah Watson and Isaac Sutton are presented in a kind of enhanced Pedigree Chart which displays the graphic representation of their direct-line ancestors and the children of the couple. This chapter contains information about the couple whose offspring are listed in the later chapters.

The chapter titled "Families of her Descendants" provides details (as known as of the publication date) for the offspring of Sarah Watson and Isaac Sutton. There is a chapter for each generation. Relatives are listed in the order of the nearness of their relationship.

Sources for the information provided are given in the footnotes.

This document reports the details of 68 individuals, of whom 38 are male and 30 are female. Of the 32 individuals with recorded birth and death dates, the average lifespan was 64.03 years. Of these, 17 males averaged 61.53 years, and 15 females averaged 66.87 years. The longest living male was Wesley Atfield Fennell (ca.1913–ca.2000), who died aged 87. The longest living female was Ann A Sutton (1878–1973), who died aged 95.

Family of the Starting Person

Family of Sarah Watson and Isaac Sutton

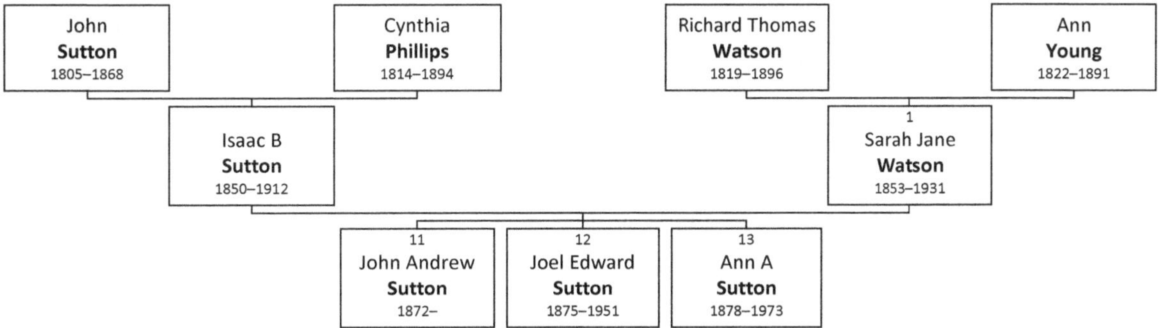

1. **Sarah Jane**[2] **Watson** was born on Wednesday, June 29, 1853, at Southwold in Elgin, Ontario, Canada.[1–10] She was the daughter of Richard Thomas Watson and Ann Young.

    Sarah Jane died in Kern, California, USA, on November 15, 1931, at the age of 78.[8, 11] She was buried at Dutton (Fairview Cemetery,   Dutton, Elgin County, Ontario, Canada) in Elgin, Ontario, Canada.[11]

---

1   Ancestry.com and The Church of Jesus Christ of Latter-day Saints, 1871 Census of Canada (Provo, UT, USA, Ancestry.com Operations Inc, 2009), Ancestry.com, Year: 1871; Census Place: Southwold, Elgin West, Ontario; Roll: C-9898; Page: 6; Family No: 24.
    [Source citation includes one media item]

2   Ancestry.com and The Church of Jesus Christ of Latter-day Saints, 1861 Census of Canada (Provo, UT, USA, Ancestry.com Operations Inc, 2009), Ancestry.com, Library and Archives Canada; Ottawa, Ontario, Canada; Census Returns For 1861; Roll: C-1019.
    [Source citation includes one media item]

3   Ancestry.com and Genealogical Research Library (Brampton, Ontario, Canada), Ontario, Canada, Marriages, 1801-1928 (Provo, UT, USA, Ancestry.com Operations, Inc., 2010), Ancestry.com, Archives of Ontario; Toronto, Ontario, Canada; Registrations of Marriages, 1869-1928; Series: MS932; Reel: 6.
    [Source citation includes one media item]

4   Ancestry.com, 1901 Census of Canada (Provo, UT, USA, Ancestry.com Operations Inc, 2006), Ancestry.com, Year: 1901; Census Place: Dutton (Village), Elgin (west/ouest), Ontario; Page: 15; Family No: 175.
    [Source citation includes one media item]

5   Ancestry.com, 1891 Census of Canada (Provo, UT, USA, Ancestry.com Operations Inc, 2008), Ancestry.com, Year: 1891; Census Place: Dunwich, Elgin West, Ontario; Roll: T-6334; Family No: 57.
    [Source citation includes one media item]

6   Ancestry.com, Detroit Border Crossings and Passenger and Crew Lists, 1905-1957 (Provo, UT, USA, Ancestry.com Operations Inc, 2006), Ancestry.com, The National Archives at Washington, D.C; Washington, D.C.; Series Title: Card Manifests (Alphabetical) of Individuals Entering through the Port of Detroit, Michigan, 1906-1954; NAI: 4527226; Record Group Title: Records of the Immigration and Naturalizatio.
    [Source citation includes one media item]

7   Ancestry.com, 1930 United States Federal Census (Provo, UT, USA, Ancestry.com Operations Inc, 2002), Ancestry.com, Year: 1930; Census Place: Bakersfield, Kern, California; Roll: 121; Page: 2A; Enumeration District: 0016; Image: 881.0; FHL microfilm: 2339856.
    [Source citation includes one media item]

8   Ancestry.com, California, Death Index, 1905-1939 (Provo, UT, USA, Ancestry.com Operations, Inc., 2013), Ancestry.com.
    [Source citation includes one media item]

9   Ancestry.com and The Church of Jesus Christ of Latter-day Saints, 1881 Census of Canada (Provo, UT, USA, Ancestry.com Operations Inc, 2009), Ancestry.com, Year: 1881; Census Place: Southwold, Elgin West, Ontario; Roll: C_13266; Page: 8; Family No: 34.
    [Source citation includes one media item]

10 Ancestry.com, 1921 Census of Canada (Provo, UT, USA, Ancestry.com Operations Inc, 2013), Ancestry.com, Reference Number: RG 31; Folder Number: 56; Census Place: 56, Elgin West, Ontario; Page Number: 4.
    [Source citation includes one media item]

11 Ancestry.com, Canada, Find A Grave Index, 1600s-Current (Provo, UT, USA, Ancestry.com Operations, Inc., 2012), Ancestry.com.

More facts and events for Sarah Jane Watson:

Residence:	1861	Elgin, Ontario, Canada[2]
		Dau / Cohab: Richard Watson 42, Ann 40, William 17, Clemington 11, Joel 9, Sarah 6, Sharlotte 6, Joshua 4, Joseph 3.
Residence:	1871	Elgin, Ontario, Canada[1]
		Cohab: Richard Watson 55, Ann Watson 57, Joel Watson 19, Sarah J Watson 18, Sharlott Watson 18, Josiah Watson 15, Joseph Watson 13.
Residence:	1881	Elgin, Ontario, Canada[9]
		Married / Cohab: Isaac Sutton 30, Jane Sutton 28, Andrew Sutton 9, Joel Sutton 6, Anna Sutton 4.
Residence:	1891	Elgin, Ontario, Canada[5]
		Married; Wife / Cohab: Isaac Sutton 41, Janes Sutton 37, Andrew Sutton 18, Joe Sutton 16, Annie Sutton 12.
Residence:	1901	Elgin, Ontario, Canada[4]
		Married; Wife / Cohab: Isac Sutton 57, Sarah J Sutton 47, Joel Sutton 26, Annie McGill 22.
Residence:	June 1, 1921	Elgin, Ontario, Canada[10]
		Methodist; Widowed; Head / Cohab: Sarh Sutton
Residence:	1930	Bakersfield, Kern, California, USA[7]
		Widowed; Alien; Mother-in-law / Cohab: Wesley R Mcgill 53, Annie L Mcgill 51, George B Mcgill 24, Sarah J Sutton 77.

They had three children: John (1872–), Joel (1875–1951) and Ann (1878–1973). Isaac B Sutton was born at Southwold, Elgin, Canada West in Canada on Friday, March 22, 1850.[2–5, 9, 12–14] He was the son of John Sutton and Cynthia Phillips.

Isaac B reached 62 years of age and died in Elgin, Ontario, Canada, on November 23, 1912.[11, 12] He was buried at Dutton (Fairview Dutton Cemetery,   10764 Currie Road   Dutton   Elgin County Ontario   Canada) in Elgin, Ontario, Canada.[11]

More facts and events for Isaac B Sutton:

Residence:	1852	Canada[13]
Residence:	1861	Elgin, Ontario, Canada[2]
		Cohab: John Sutton 53, Cynthia 47, Calvin 20, Elijah 18, Fred 16, Isaac 12, Angus 3.
Residence:	about 1871	Elgin, Ontario, Canada[14]
		Cohab: Cyntha Sutton 51, Isaac Sutton 21, Agnes Sutton 13.
Residence:	1881	Elgin, Ontario, Canada[9]
		Married; Farmer / Cohab: Isaac Sutton 30, Jane Sutton 28, Andrew Sutton 9, Joel Sutton 6, Anna Sutton 4.
Residence:	1891	Elgin, Ontario, Canada[5]

[12] Ancestry.com, Ontario, Canada, Deaths, 1869-1938 and Deaths Overseas, 1939-1947 (Provo, UT, USA, Ancestry.com Operations Inc, 2010), Ancestry.com, Archives of Ontario; Toronto, Ontario, Canada; Series: MS935; Reel: 174.
[Source citation includes one media item]

[13] Ancestry.com, 1851 Census of Canada East, Canada West, New Brunswick, and Nova Scotia (Provo, UT, USA, Ancestry.com Operations Inc, 2006), Ancestry.com, Year: 1851; Census Place: Southwold, Elgin County, Canada West (Ontario); Schedule: A; Roll: C_11719; Page: 7; Line: 5.
[Source citation includes one media item]

[14] Ancestry.com and The Church of Jesus Christ of Latter-day Saints, 1871 Census of Canada (Provo, UT, USA, Ancestry.com Operations Inc, 2009), Ancestry.com, Year: 1871; Census Place: Southwold, Elgin West, Ontario; Roll: C-9898; Page: 6.
[Source citation includes one media item]

Married;   Head; Farmer / Cohab: Isaac Sutton 41,   Janes Sutton 37,   Andrew Sutton 18,   Joe Sutton 16,   Annie Sutton 12.

Residence: 1901   Elgin, Ontario, Canada[4]

Married; Head; Engineer / Cohab: Isac Sutton 57,   Sarah J Sutton 47,   Joel Sutton 26,   Annie McGill 22.

Figure 1: Fairview Cemetery - Dutton

Figure 2: Isaac Sutton Headstone

Families of her Descendants

Family of John Sutton and Mary Dake

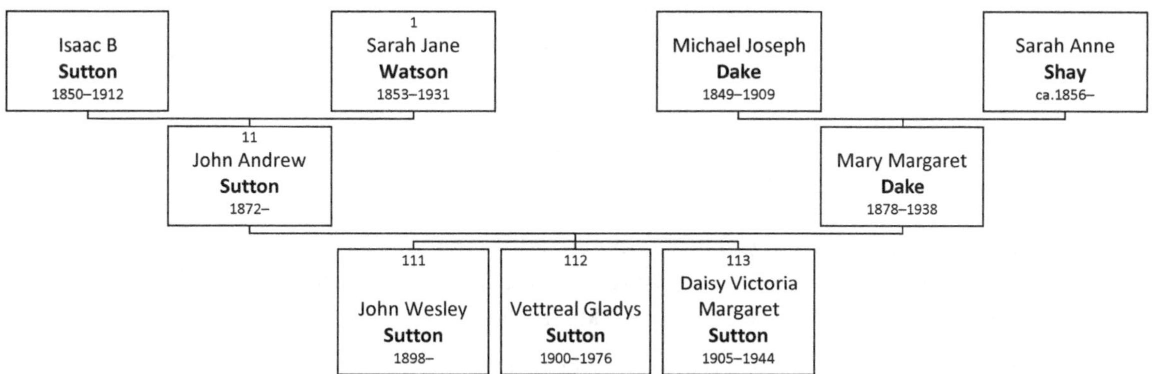

11. **John Andrew[3] Sutton** was born on Saturday, June 1, 1872, in Elgin, Ontario, Canada.[15–20] He was the son of Isaac B Sutton and Sarah Jane Watson (1).

More facts and events for John Andrew Sutton:

Residence:	1881	Elgin, Ontario, Canada[19]
		Cohab: Isaac Sutton 30, Jane Sutton 28, Andrew Sutton 9, Joel Sutton 6, Anna Sutton 4.
Residence:	1891	Elgin, Ontario, Canada[15]
		Single; Son / Cohab: Isaac Sutton 41, Janes Sutton 37, Andrew Sutton 18, Joe Sutton 16, Annie Sutton 12.
Residence:	1901	Elgin, Ontario, Canada[20]
		Married; Head; Engineer / Cohab: John A Sutton 28, Mary M Sutton 23, John W Sutton 2, Vectreal G Sutton 1.
Residence:	1916	Brandon, Manitoba, Canada[18]
		Married; Self; Boarding House / Cohab: John Andrew Sutton 45, Mary Margaret Sutton 38, John Wesley Sutton 17, Vettreal Gladys Sutton 15, Daisy Victoria

15   Ancestry.com, 1891 Census of Canada (Provo, UT, USA, Ancestry.com Operations Inc, 2008), Ancestry.com, Year: 1891; Census Place: Dunwich, Elgin West, Ontario; Roll: T-6334; Family No: 57.
[Source citation includes one media item]

16   Ancestry.com and Genealogical Research Library (Brampton, Ontario, Canada), Ontario, Canada, Marriages, 1801-1928 (Provo, UT, USA, Ancestry.com Operations, Inc., 2010), Ancestry.com, Archives of Ontario; Toronto, Ontario, Canada; Registrations of Marriages, 1869-1928; Series: MS932; Reel: 92.
[Source citation includes one media item]

17   Ancestry.com, 1921 Census of Canada (Provo, UT, USA, Ancestry.com Operations Inc, 2013), Ancestry.com, Reference Number: RG 31; Folder Number: 29; Census Place: Winnipeg (City), Winnipeg Centre, Manitoba; Page Number: 1.
[Source citation includes one media item]

18   Ancestry.com and The Church of Jesus Christ of Latter-day Saints, 1916 Canada Census of Manitoba, Saskatchewan, and Alberta (Provo, UT, USA, Ancestry.com Operations Inc, 2009), Ancestry.com, Year: 1916; Census Place: Manitoba, Brandon, 06; Roll: T-21925; Page: 14; Family No: 126.
[Source citation includes one media item]

19   Ancestry.com and The Church of Jesus Christ of Latter-day Saints, 1881 Census of Canada (Provo, UT, USA, Ancestry.com Operations Inc, 2009), Ancestry.com, Year: 1881; Census Place: Southwold, Elgin West, Ontario; Roll: C_13266; Page: 8; Family No: 34.
[Source citation includes one media item]

20   Ancestry.com, 1901 Census of Canada (Provo, UT, USA, Ancestry.com Operations Inc, 2006), Ancestry.com, Year: 1901; Census Place: Dutton (Village), Elgin (west/ouest), Ontario; Page: 15; Family No: 174.
[Source citation includes one media item]

Sutton 11.

| Residence: | June 1, 1921 | Winnipeg, Manitoba, Canada[17] |

Residence: June 1, 1921   Winnipeg, Manitoba, Canada[17]
    Marital Status: Married; Relation to Head of House: Head

Residence: 1935   Winnipeg, Manitoba, Canada[21]
    Name: John A Sutton / Address: 458 Balmoral / Occupation: retired /
    Cohabitation: Mrs John A Sutton, John Sutton (Mechanic)

Residence: 1945   Winnipeg, Manitoba, Canada[21]
    Name: John Andrew Sutton / Address: 458 Balmoral / Occupation: retired /
    Cohabitation: John Wesley Sutton (Mechanic)

They had three children: John (1898–), Vettreal (1900–1976) and Daisy (1905–1944). Mary Margaret Dake was born in Hamilton, Ontario, Canada, on Friday, January 11, 1878.[16–18, 20, 22–23] She was the daughter of Michael Joseph Dake and Sarah Anne Shay.

Mary Margaret reached 60 years of age and died in Winnipeg, Manitoba, Canada, on December 12, 1938.[23]

More facts and events for Mary Margaret Dake:

Residence: 1891   Elgin, Ontario, Canada[22]
    Single;   Dau / Cohab: Michael J Dake 42,   Sarah A Dake 32,   Joseph L Dake 16,   Edward V Dake 15,   Maggie M Dake 13,   John Lewis Dake 11,   Annie E Dake 9,   James M Dake 7,   William L Dake 1.

Residence: 1901   Elgin, Ontario, Canada[20]
    Married;   Wife / Cohab: John A Sutton 28,   Mary M Sutton 23,   John W Sutton 2,   Vectreal G Sutton 1.

Residence: 1916   Brandon, Manitoba, Canada[18]
    Married;   Wife / Cohab: John Andrew Sutton 45,   Mary Margaret Sutton 38,   John Wesley Sutton 17,   Vettreal Gladys Sutton 15,   Daisy Victoria Sutton 11.

Residence: June 1, 1921   Winnipeg, Manitoba, Canada[17]
    Married; Wife / Cohab: John Andrew Sutton 48,   Mary Margaret Sutton 43,   John Wesley Sutton 23,   Vettreal Gladys Sutton 20,   Daisy Victoria Sutter 16,   Benjamin Miller 23.

---

[21]   Ancestry.com, Canada, Voters Lists, 1935-1980 (Provo, UT, USA, Ancestry.com Operations, Inc., 2012), Ancestry.com.
[Source citation includes one media item]

[22]   Ancestry.com, 1891 Census of Canada (Provo, UT, USA, Ancestry.com Operations Inc, 2008), Ancestry.com, Year: 1891; Census Place: Southwold, Elgin West, Ontario; Roll: T-6334; Family No: 266.
[Source citation includes one media item]

[23]   Ancestry.com, Web: Manitoba, Death Index, 1881-1941 (Provo, UT, USA, Ancestry.com Operations, Inc., 2012), Ancestry.com, Manitoba Consumer and Corporate Affairs; Manitoba, Canada.

Figure 3: The Death of Jumbo the Elephant Story
(September 15, 1885)
Jumbo died at a railway classification yard following a
Barnum and Bailey circus performance in St Thomas.

John Sutton

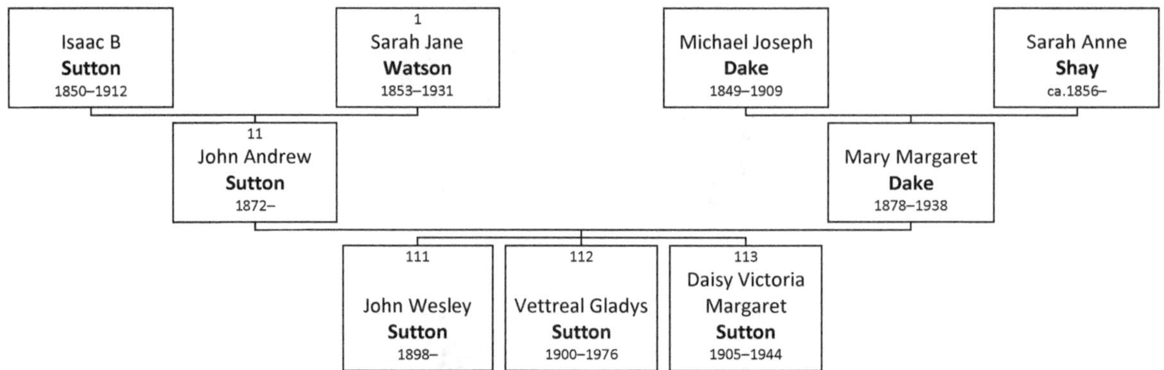

111.   **John Wesley**[4] **Sutton** was born on Saturday, July 9, 1898, in Elgin, Ontario, Canada.[24–27] He was the son of John Andrew Sutton (11) and Mary Margaret Dake.

John Wesley served in the military on February 15, 1942.[28] He served in the military on July 31, 1945.[29]

More facts and events for John Wesley Sutton:

Residence:	1901	Elgin, Ontario, Canada[26]
		Single; Son / Cohab: John A Sutton 28, Mary M Sutton 23, John W Sutton 2, Vectreal G Sutton 1.
Residence:	1916	Brandon, Manitoba, Canada[25]
		Single; Son / Cohab: John Andrew Sutton 45, Mary Margaret Sutton 38, John Wesley Sutton 17, Vettreal Gladys Sutton 15, Daisy Victoria Sutton 11.
Residence:	June 1, 1921	Winnipeg, Manitoba, Canada[24]
		Marital Status: Single; Relation to Head of House: Son
Residence:	1940	Winnipeg, Manitoba, Canada[30]
		Name: John W Sutton / Address: 458 Balmoral / Occupation: labourer / Cohabitation: J A Sutton (Mechanic)

[24]   Ancestry.com, 1921 Census of Canada (Provo, UT, USA, Ancestry.com Operations Inc, 2013), Ancestry.com, Reference Number: RG 31; Folder Number: 29; Census Place: Winnipeg (City), Winnipeg Centre, Manitoba; Page Number: 1.
[Source citation includes one media item]

[25]   Ancestry.com and The Church of Jesus Christ of Latter-day Saints, 1916 Canada Census of Manitoba, Saskatchewan, and Alberta (Provo, UT, USA, Ancestry.com Operations Inc, 2009), Ancestry.com, Year: 1916; Census Place: Manitoba, Brandon, 06; Roll: T-21925; Page: 14; Family No: 126.
[Source citation includes one media item]

[26]   Ancestry.com, 1901 Census of Canada (Provo, UT, USA, Ancestry.com Operations Inc, 2006), Ancestry.com, Year: 1901; Census Place: Dutton (Village), Elgin (west/ouest), Ontario; Page: 15; Family No: 174.
[Source citation includes one media item]

[27]   Ancestry.com, Ontario, Canada Births, 1869-1913 (Provo, UT, USA, Ancestry.com Operations Inc, 2010), Ancestry.com, Archives of Ontario; Series: MS929; Reel: 142.
[Source citation includes one media item]

[28]   Ancestry.com, UK, Allied Prisoners of War, 1939-1945 (Lehi, UT, USA, Ancestry.com Operations, Inc., 2018), Ancestry.com, The National Archives; Kew, London, England; WO 392 POW Lists 1943-1945; Reference Number: WO 392/26.

[29]   Ancestry.com, U.S. World War II Navy Muster Rolls, 1938-1949 (Provo, UT, USA, Ancestry.com Operations Inc, 2011), Ancestry.com, National Archives at College Park; College Park, Maryland, United States; Muster Rolls of U.S. Navy Ships, Stations, and Other Naval Activities, 01/01/1939 - 01/01/1949; Record Group: 24, Records of the Bureau of Naval Personnel, 1798 - 2007; Series ARC ID.
[Source citation includes one media item]

[30]   Ancestry.com, Canada, Voters Lists, 1935-1980 (Provo, UT, USA, Ancestry.com Operations, Inc., 2012), Ancestry.com.
[Source citation includes one media item]

Residence: 1945   Winnipeg, Manitoba, Canada[30]
Name: John W Sutton / Address: 458 Balmoral / Occupation: mechanic /
Cohabitation: John Andrew Sutton (retired)

Family of Vettreal Sutton and Benjamin Miller

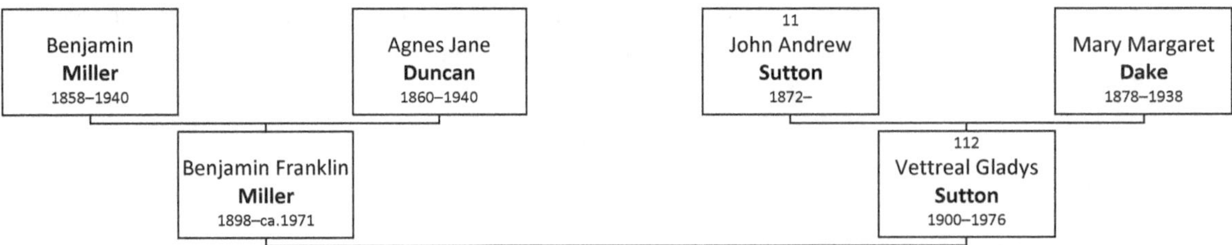

112.   **Vettreal Gladys[4] Sutton** was born on Friday, August 10, 1900, in Elgin, Ontario, Canada.[31–34] She was the daughter of John Andrew Sutton (11) and Mary Margaret Dake.

Vettreal Gladys died in Winnipeg, Manitoba, Canada, on December 13, 1976, at the age of 76.[35] She was buried in Winnipeg, Manitoba, Canada.[35]

More facts and events for Vettreal Gladys Sutton:

Residence:	1901	Elgin, Ontario, Canada[33]
		Single; Dau / Cohab: John A Sutton 28, Mary M Sutton 23, John W Sutton 2, Vectreal G Sutton 1.
Residence:	1916	Brandon, Manitoba, Canada[32]
		Single; Dau / Cohab: John Andrew Sutton 45, Mary Margaret Sutton 38, John Wesley Sutton 17, Vettreal Gladys Sutton 15, Daisy Victoria Sutton 11.
Residence:	June 1, 1921	Winnipeg, Manitoba, Canada[31]
		Single; Dau; Broker / Cohab: John Andrew Sutton 48, Mary Margaret Sutton 43, John Wesley Sutton 23, Vettreal Gladys Sutton 20, Daisy Victoria Sutter 16, Benjamin Miller 23.
Residence:	1963	Winnipeg, Manitoba, Canada[36]

Benjamin Franklin Miller was born in Lanark, Ontario, Canada, on Tuesday, April 12, 1898.[37–42] He was the son of Benjamin Miller and Agnes Jane Duncan.

31   Ancestry.com, 1921 Census of Canada (Provo, UT, USA, Ancestry.com Operations Inc, 2013), Ancestry.com, Reference Number: RG 31; Folder Number: 29; Census Place: Winnipeg (City), Winnipeg Centre, Manitoba; Page Number: 1.
[Source citation includes one media item]

32   Ancestry.com and The Church of Jesus Christ of Latter-day Saints, 1916 Canada Census of Manitoba, Saskatchewan, and Alberta (Provo, UT, USA, Ancestry.com Operations Inc, 2009), Ancestry.com, Year: 1916; Census Place: Manitoba, Brandon, 06; Roll: T-21925; Page: 14; Family No: 126.
[Source citation includes one media item]

33   Ancestry.com, 1901 Census of Canada (Provo, UT, USA, Ancestry.com Operations Inc, 2006), Ancestry.com, Year: 1901; Census Place: Dutton (Village), Elgin (west/ouest), Ontario; Page: 15; Family No: 174.
[Source citation includes one media item]

34   Ancestry.com, Ontario, Canada Births, 1869-1913 (Provo, UT, USA, Ancestry.com Operations Inc, 2010), Ancestry.com, Archives of Ontario; Toronto, Ontario, Canada; Registrations of Births and Stillbirths, 1869-1913; Series: MS929; Reel: 149; Record Group: RG 80-2.
[Source citation includes one media item]

35   Ancestry.com, Canada, Find A Grave Index, 1600s-Current (Provo, UT, USA, Ancestry.com Operations, Inc., 2012), Ancestry.com.

36   Ancestry.com, Canada, Voters Lists, 1935-1980 (Provo, UT, USA, Ancestry.com Operations, Inc., 2012), Ancestry.com, Library and Archives Canada; Ottawa, Ontario, Canada; Voters Lists, Federal Elections, 1935-1980.
[Source citation includes one media item]

37   Ancestry.com, 1911 Census of Canada (Provo, UT, USA, Ancestry.com Operations Inc, 2006), Ancestry.com, Year: 1911; Census Place: 18, Brandon, Manitoba; Page: 4; Family No: 24.
[Source citation includes one media item]

Benjamin Franklin reached 72 years of age and died at (Likely) in Winnipeg, Manitoba, Canada, about 1971.

More facts and events for Benjamin Franklin Miller:

Residence:	1901	Brandon, Manitoba, Canada[39]
		Single; Son / Cohab: Binjamin Miller 42, Agnes J Miller 41, Evered J Miller 15, Ethel J Miller 14, Nellie M Miller 12, Carrie A Milles 10, Anna W Milles 8, Russel D Milles 6, William Milles 4, Benjiman Milles 3, Carman C Milles 1.
Residence:	July 21, 1906	Brandon, Manitoba, Canada[38]
		Single; Son / Cohab: Bengamin Miller 48, Agnes 46, Evered J 21, Ethel 19, Nellie M 17, Carrie A 15, Anna W 13, Russel D 11, William M 9, Benjamin F 8, Carman C 6, Edith M 3, Mauew 19.
Residence:	1911	Brandon, Manitoba, Canada[37]
		Single; Son / Cohab: Benjamin Miller 53, Agnes J Miller 51, Nellis Miller 23, Russel D Miller 16, William H Miller 14, Benjamin F Miller 12, Corman C Miller 10, Margret E Miller 8, Marion E Miller 6.
Residence:	1916	Brandon, Manitoba, Canada[40]
		Single; Son / Cohab: Benjamin Miller 58, Agnes Miller 56, Carey A Miller 25, Russel Miller 21, William Miller 19, Frank Miller 18, Herman Miller 16, Margaret Miller 12, Marion Miller 10, Loylld Gemmel 18.
Residence:	June 1, 1921	Winnipeg, Manitoba, Canada[41]
		Methodist; Single; Lodger; Bookkeeper / Cohab: John Andrew Sutton 48, Mary Margaret Sutton 43, John Wesley Sutton 23, Vettreal Gladys Sutton [eventual wife] 20, Daisy Victoria Sutter 16, Benjamin Miller 23.
Residence:	1940	Reston, Manitoba, Canada[36]
		Cohab: Benjamin Franklin (farmer), Mrs Ben Miller
Residence:	1962	Winnipeg, Manitoba, Canada[36]
		Warehouseman

38   Ancestry.com, 1906 Canada Census of Manitoba, Saskatchewan, and Alberta (Provo, UT, USA, Ancestry.com Operations Inc, 2006), Ancestry.com, Year: 1906; Census Place: 06, Brandon, Manitoba; Page: 36; Family No: 239.
[Source citation includes one media item]

39   Ancestry.com, 1901 Census of Canada (Provo, UT, USA, Ancestry.com Operations Inc, 2006), Ancestry.com, Year: 1901; Census Place: Pipestone, Brandon, Manitoba; Page: 2; Family No: 15.
[Source citation includes one media item]

40   Ancestry.com and The Church of Jesus Christ of Latter-day Saints, 1916 Canada Census of Manitoba, Saskatchewan, and Alberta (Provo, UT, USA, Ancestry.com Operations Inc, 2009), Ancestry.com, Year: 1916; Census Place: Manitoba, Brandon, 06; Roll: T-21925; Page: 12; Family No: 107.
[Source citation includes one media item]

41   Ancestry.com, 1921 Census of Canada (Provo, UT, USA, Ancestry.com Operations Inc, 2013), Ancestry.com, Reference Number: RG 31; Folder Number: 29; Census Place: 29, Winnipeg Centre, Manitoba; Page Number: 2.
[Source citation includes one media item]

42   Ancestry.com, Ontario, Canada Births, 1869-1913 (Provo, UT, USA, Ancestry.com Operations Inc, 2010), Ancestry.com, Archives of Ontario; Toronto, Ontario, Canada; Registrations of Births and Stillbirths, 1869-1913; Series: MS929; Reel: 142; Record Group: RG 80-2.
[Source citation includes one media item]

Figure 4: Elmwood Cemetery

Family of Daisy Sutton and Neil McLeod

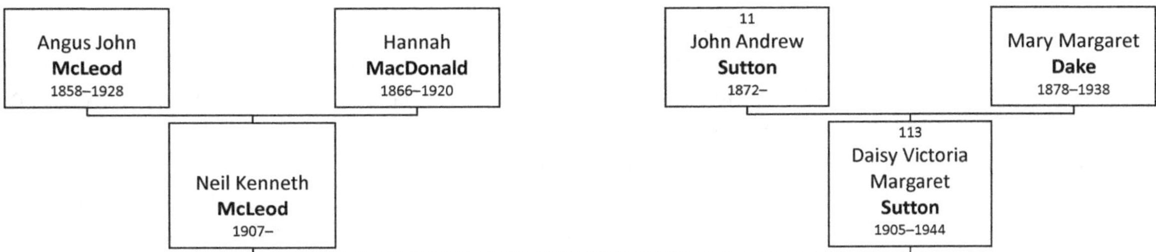

113. **Daisy Victoria Margaret[4] Sutton** was born on Monday, April 3, 1905, at Dutton in Elgin, Ontario, Canada.[43–46] She was the daughter of John Andrew Sutton (11) and Mary Margaret Dake.

Daisy Victoria Margaret died at (Likely) in Winnipeg, Manitoba, Canada, in November 1944 at the age of 39.[47] She was buried at Elmwood Cemetery,   Winnipeg, Greater Winnipeg, Manitoba, Canada,   PLOT: 11-G0083 in Winnipeg, Manitoba, Canada.[47]

More facts and events for Daisy Victoria Margaret Sutton:

Residence:	1901	Elgin, Ontario, Canada[46]
		Single; Dau / Cohab: John A Sutton 28, Mary M Sutton 23, John W Sutton 2, Vectreal G Sutton 1.
Residence:	1916	Brandon, Manitoba, Canada[44]
		Single; Dau / Cohab: John Andrew Sutton 45, Mary Margaret Sutton 38, John Wesley Sutton 17, Vettreal Gladys Sutton 15, Daisy Victoria Sutton 11.
Residence:	June 1, 1921	Winnipeg, Manitoba, Canada[43]
		Single; Dau; Bookkeeper, Dep't Store / Cohab: John Andrew Sutton 48, Mary Margaret Sutton 43, John Wesley Sutton 23, Vettreal Gladys Sutton 20, Daisy Victoria Sutter 16, Benjamin Miller 23.

Neil Kenneth McLeod was born in Winnipeg, Manitoba, Canada, on Wednesday, January 23, 1907.[48–51] He is the son of Angus John McLeod and Hannah MacDonald.

---

43   Ancestry.com, 1921 Census of Canada (Provo, UT, USA, Ancestry.com Operations Inc, 2013), Ancestry.com, Reference Number: RG 31; Folder Number: 29; Census Place: Winnipeg (City), Winnipeg Centre, Manitoba; Page Number: 2.
[Source citation includes one media item]

44   Ancestry.com and The Church of Jesus Christ of Latter-day Saints, 1916 Canada Census of Manitoba, Saskatchewan, and Alberta (Provo, UT, USA, Ancestry.com Operations Inc, 2009), Ancestry.com, Year: 1916; Census Place: Manitoba, Brandon, 06; Roll: T-21925; Page: 14; Family No: 126.
[Source citation includes one media item]

45   Ancestry.com, Ontario, Canada Births, 1869-1913 (Provo, UT, USA, Ancestry.com Operations Inc, 2010), Ancestry.com, Archives of Ontario; Series: MS929; Reel: 171.
[Source citation includes one media item]

46   Ancestry.com, 1901 Census of Canada (Provo, UT, USA, Ancestry.com Operations Inc, 2006), Ancestry.com, Year: 1901; Census Place: Dutton (Village), Elgin (west/ouest), Ontario; Page: 15; Family No: 174.
[Source citation includes one media item]

47   Ancestry.com, Canada, Find A Grave Index, 1600s-Current (Provo, UT, USA, Ancestry.com Operations, Inc., 2012), Ancestry.com.

48   Ancestry.com, Web: Manitoba, Birth Index, 1866-1912 (Provo, UT, USA, Ancestry.com Operations, Inc., 2013), Ancestry.com, Manitoba Consumer and Corporate Affairs; Manitoba, Canada.

49   Ancestry.com and The Church of Jesus Christ of Latter-day Saints, 1916 Canada Census of Manitoba, Saskatchewan, and Alberta (Provo, UT, USA, Ancestry.com Operations Inc, 2009), Ancestry.com, Year: 1916; Census Place: Manitoba, Winnipeg Centre, 14; Roll: T-21932; Page: 3; Family No: 40.
[Source citation includes one media item]

More facts and events for Neil Kenneth McLeod:

Residence: 1916   Winnipeg, Manitoba, Canada[49]
                          Single;   Son / Cohab: Angus Mcleod 56,   Hannah Mcleod 47,   Malcolm Mcleod
                          30,   James H Mcleod 27,   William Mcleod 25,   Lena Mcleod 20,   Jessie W
                          Mcleod 17,   Donald Mcleod 13,   Kennie Mcleod 8,   Alexander Guthrie 35.
Residence: June 1, 1921 Winnipeg, Manitoba, Canada[51]
                          Single; Son; Farmer / Cohab: Angus McLeod 62,   Malcolm (s) 36,   James   (s)
                          34,   William (s) 32,   Edith (d-in-l) 28,   William (gs) 3,   Edith (gd) 1, Donald (s)
                          18, Kenneth (s) 15, Christina HIlby (d) 24, Ernest Hilby   (s-in-l), William Bowden
                          (boarder).

Figure 5: Elmwood Cemetery

50   Ancestry.com, U.S. WWII Draft Cards Young Men, 1940-1947 (Provo, UT, USA, Ancestry.com Operations, Inc., 2011), Ancestry.com, The
     National Archives in St. Louis, Missouri; St. Louis, Missouri; WWII Draft Registration Cards for Illinois, 10/16/1940-03/31/1947; Record Group:
     Records of the Selective Service System, 147; Box: 1182.
     [Source citation includes one media item]

51   Ancestry.com, 1921 Census of Canada (Provo, UT, USA, Ancestry.com Operations Inc, 2013), Ancestry.com, Reference Number: RG 31; Folder
     Number: 29; Census Place: 29, Winnipeg Centre, Manitoba; Page Number: 41.
     [Source citation includes one media item]

Family of Joel Sutton and Ellen Grosbeck

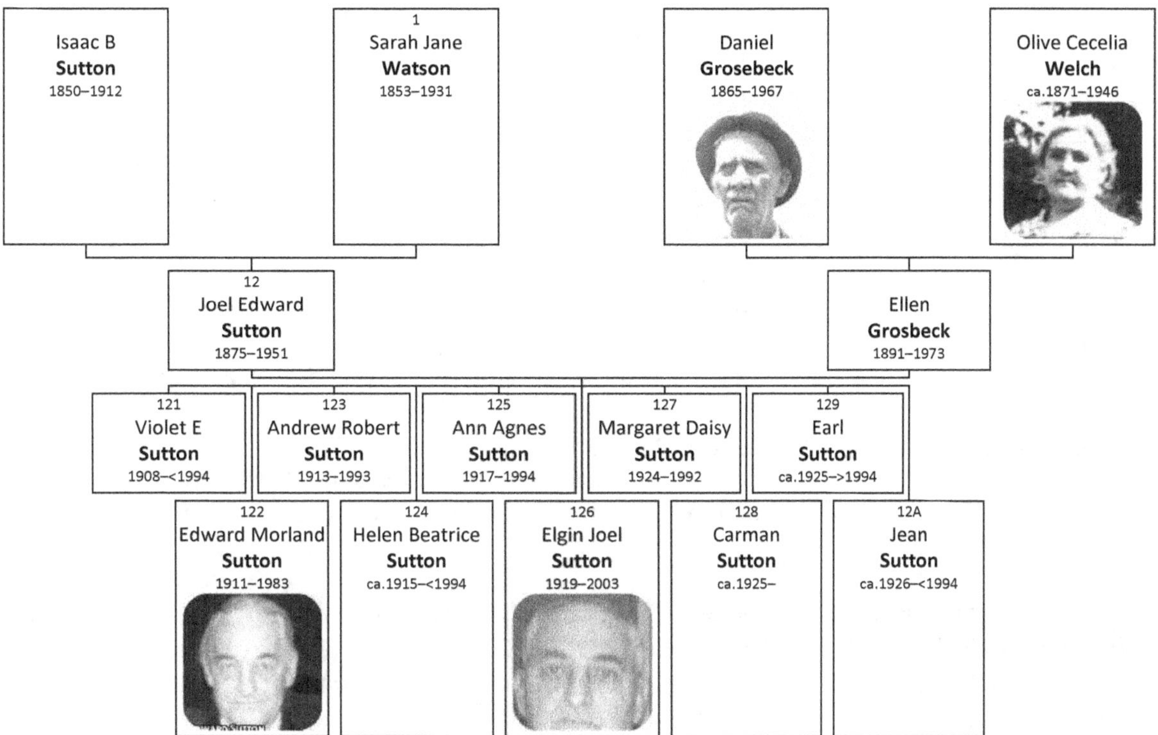

12. **Joel Edward[3] Sutton** was born on Friday, February 12, 1875, in Elgin, Ontario, Canada.[52–59] He was the son of Isaac B Sutton and Sarah Jane Watson (1).

Joel Edward died in Ontario, Canada, on September 19, 1951, at the age of 76.[60] He was buried at Dutton (Fairview Cemetery - Dutton,   Dutton   Elgin County   Ontario, Canada) in Elgin, Ontario, Canada.[60]

52 Ancestry.com, 1901 Census of Canada (Provo, UT, USA, Ancestry.com Operations Inc, 2006), Ancestry.com, Year: 1901; Census Place: Dutton (Village), Elgin (west/ouest), Ontario; Page: 15; Family No: 175.
[Source citation includes one media item]

53 Ancestry.com, 1891 Census of Canada (Provo, UT, USA, Ancestry.com Operations Inc, 2008), Ancestry.com, Year: 1891; Census Place: Dunwich, Elgin West, Ontario; Roll: T-6334; Family No: 57.
[Source citation includes one media item]

54 Ancestry.com, 1921 Census of Canada (Provo, UT, USA, Ancestry.com Operations Inc, 2013), Ancestry.com, Reference Number: RG 31; Folder Number: 56; Census Place: Dutton (Town), Elgin West, Ontario; Page Number: 8.
[Source citation includes one media item]

55 Ancestry.com and The Church of Jesus Christ of Latter-day Saints, 1881 Census of Canada (Provo, UT, USA, Ancestry.com Operations Inc, 2009), Ancestry.com, Year: 1881; Census Place: Southwold, Elgin West, Ontario; Roll: C_13266; Page: 8; Family No: 34.
[Source citation includes one media item]

56 Ancestry.com, 1911 Census of Canada (Provo, UT, USA, Ancestry.com Operations Inc, 2006), Ancestry.com, Year: 1911; Census Place: 39 - Dutton, Elgin West, Ontario; Page: 17; Family No: 217.
[Source citation includes one media item]

57 Ancestry.com, Canada, Soldiers of the First World War, 1914-1918 (Provo, UT, USA, Ancestry.com Operations, Inc., 2006), Ancestry.com.
[Source citation includes one media item]

58 Ancestry.com, U.S., Social Security Applications and Claims Index, 1936-2007 (Provo, UT, USA, Ancestry.com Operations, Inc., 2015), Ancestry.com.

59 Ancestry.com, U.S., Railroad Retirement Pension Index, 1934-1987 (Lehi, UT, USA, Ancestry.com Operations, Inc., 2017), Ancestry.com, The National Archives at Atlanta; Morrow, Georgia; Records of the Railroad Retirement Board, 1934 - 1987; Record Group Number: 184.

60 Ancestry.com, Canada, Find A Grave Index, 1600s-Current (Provo, UT, USA, Ancestry.com Operations, Inc., 2012), Ancestry.com.

More facts and events for Joel Edward Sutton:

Residence:	1881	Elgin, Ontario, Canada[55]

Cohab: Isaac Sutton 30, Jane Sutton 28, Andrew Sutton 9, Joel Sutton 6, Anna Sutton 4.

Residence:	1891	Elgin, Ontario, Canada[53]

Single; Son / Cohab: Isaac Sutton 41, Janes Sutton 37, Andrew Sutton 18, Joe Sutton 16, Annie Sutton 12.

Residence:	1901	Elgin, Ontario, Canada[52]

Single; Son / Cohab: Isac Sutton 57, Sarah J Sutton 47, Joel Sutton 26, Annie McGill 22.

Residence:	1911	Elgin, Ontario, Canada[56]

Married; Head / Cohab: Joel Sutton 38, Ellen Sutton 21, Violet Sutton 2, Edward Sutton 3m.

Residence:	June 1, 1921	Elgin, Ontario, Canada[54]

Married; Head; Railway Labourer / Cohab: Joel Sutton 46, Ellen Sutton 30, Violet Sutton 13, Eddie Sutton 10, Andrew Sutton 8, Helen Sutton 6, Annie Sutton 4, E Lyin Sutton 2.

They had ten children: Violet (1908–<1994), Edward (1911–1983), Andrew (1913–1993), Helen (ca.1915–<1994), Ann (1917–1994), Elgin (1919–2003), Margaret (1924–1992), Carman (ca.1925–), Earl (ca.1925–>1994) and Jean (ca.1926–<1994). Ellen Grosbeck was born at Dutton in Elgin, Ontario, Canada, on Saturday, December 26, 1891.[54, 56, 61, 62] She was the daughter of Daniel Grosebeck and Olive Cecelia Welch.

Ellen reached 81 years of age and died in St Thomas, Elgin, Ontario, Canada, in 1973.

More facts and events for Ellen Grosbeck:

Residence:	1891	Middlesex, Ontario, Canada[61]

Single; Dau / Cohab: Daniel Grosbick 23, Olive Grosbick 21, Elen Grosbick , Emley Grosbick 60.

Residence:	1901	Glencoe, Middlesex, Ontario, Canada[62]

Single; Dau / Cohab: Daniel Grosbeck 31, Olive E Grosbeck 29, Ellen Grosbeck 10, Bella Grosbeck 8, Rachal A Grosbeck 4, William H Grosbeck 2, Mary E Grosbeck 2/12.

Residence:	1911	Elgin, Ontario, Canada[56]

Married; Wife / Cohab: Joel Sutton 38, Ellen Sutton 21, Violet Sutton 2, Edward Sutton 3m.

Residence:	June 1, 1921	Elgin, Ontario, Canada[54]

Married; Wife / Cohab: Joel Sutton 46, Ellen Sutton 30, Violet Sutton 13, Eddie Sutton 10, Andrew Sutton 8, Helen Sutton 6, Annie Sutton 4, E Lyin Sutton 2.

Residence:	1949	Elgin, Ontario, Canada[63]

[61] Ancestry.com, 1891 Census of Canada (Provo, UT, USA, Ancestry.com Operations Inc, 2008), Ancestry.com, Year: 1891; Census Place: Mosa, Middlesex West, Ontario; Roll: T-6354; Family No: 66.
[Source citation includes one media item]

[62] Ancestry.com, 1901 Census of Canada (Provo, UT, USA, Ancestry.com Operations Inc, 2006), Ancestry.com, Year: 1901; Census Place: Glencoe (Village), Middlesex (west/ouest), Ontario; Page: 5; Family No: 49.
[Source citation includes one media item]

[63] Ancestry.com, Canada, Voters Lists, 1935-1980 (Provo, UT, USA, Ancestry.com Operations, Inc., 2012), Ancestry.com.
[Source citation includes one media item]

Figure 6: Fairview Cemetery - Dutton

Figure 7: Joel Edward Sutton Headstone

Violet Sutton

121.   **Violet E[4] Sutton** was born on Thursday, July 16, 1908, at Dutton in Elgin, Ontario, Canada.[64–67] She was the daughter of Joel Edward Sutton (12) and Ellen Grosbeck.

Violet E died at (Likely) in Elgin, Ontario, Canada, before 1994. Cited as Violet Vernor and as deceased in sister Ann Sutton's obituary.

More facts and events for Violet E Sutton:

Residence: 1911   Elgin, Ontario, Canada[65]
Single;   Dau / Cohab: Joel Sutton 38,   Ellen Sutton 21,   Violet Sutton 2, Edward Sutton 3m.

Residence: June 1, 1921   Elgin, Ontario, Canada[64]
Single;   Dau / Cohab: Joel Sutton 46,   Ellen Sutton 30,   Violet Sutton 13, Eddie Sutton 10,   Andrew Sutton 8,   Helen Sutton 6,   Annie Sutton 4,   E Lyin Sutton 2.

Marriages with Earl Truman Atkinson and (unknown given name) Vernor (Page 28) are known.

[64]   Ancestry.com, 1921 Census of Canada (Provo, UT, USA, Ancestry.com Operations Inc, 2013), Ancestry.com, Reference Number: RG 31; Folder Number: 56; Census Place: Dutton (Town), Elgin West, Ontario; Page Number: 8.
[Source citation includes one media item]

[65]   Ancestry.com, 1911 Census of Canada (Provo, UT, USA, Ancestry.com Operations Inc, 2006), Ancestry.com, Year: 1911; Census Place: 39 - Dutton, Elgin West, Ontario; Page: 17; Family No: 217.
[Source citation includes one media item]

[66]   Ancestry.com, Ontario, Canada Births, 1869-1913 (Provo, UT, USA, Ancestry.com Operations Inc, 2010), Ancestry.com, Archives of Ontario; Series: MS929; Reel: 4.
[Source citation includes one media item]

[67]   Ancestry.com and Genealogical Research Library (Brampton, Ontario, Canada), Ontario, Canada, Marriages, 1801-1928 (Provo, UT, USA, Ancestry.com Operations, Inc., 2010), Ancestry.com, Archives of Ontario; Toronto, Ontario, Canada; Registrations of Marriages, 1869-1928; Series: MS932; Reel: 861.
[Source citation includes one media item]

Family of Violet Sutton and Earl Atkinson

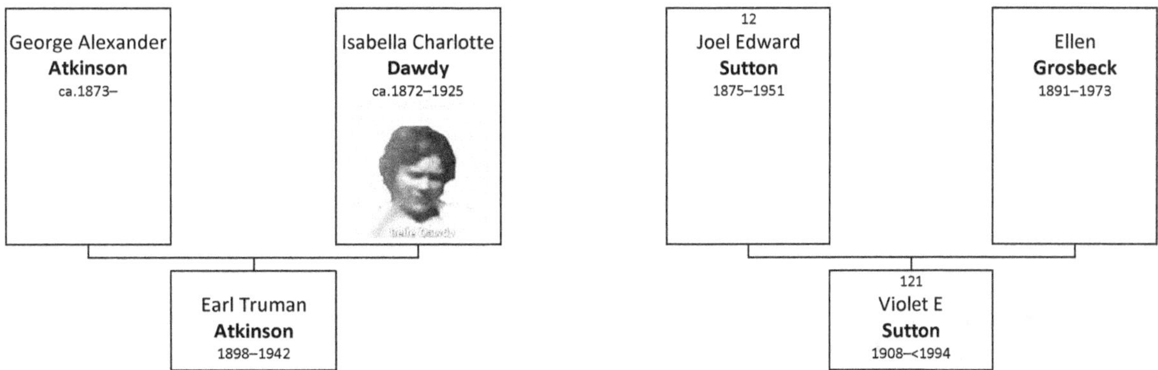

Here are the details about **Violet E Sutton's** first marriage with Earl Truman Atkinson. You can read more about Violet E on page 26.

Earl Truman Atkinson was born in St Thomas, Elgin, Ontario, Canada, on Wednesday, July 13, 1898.[67–72] He was the son of George Alexander Atkinson and Isabella Charlotte Dawdy.

Earl Truman reached 43 years of age and died at Died from Coronary Thrombosis in St Thomas, Elgin, Ontario, Canada, on June 3, 1942.[71]

More facts and events for Earl Truman Atkinson:

Residence: about 1919   St Thomas, Elgin, Ontario, Canada[68, 70]
Relation To Head: Mother
Residence: June 1, 1921   St Thomas, Elgin, Ontario, Canada[72]
Methodist; Single;   Son / Cohab: Bell Atkison (Head) 42,   Norman F Atkison (s) 24,   Trueman E Atkison (s) 2.

68   Ancestry.com, Canada, WWI CEF Personnel Files, 1914-1918 (Lehi, UT, USA, Ancestry.com Operations, Inc., 2016), Ancestry.com, Library and Archives Canada; Ottawa, Ontario, Canada; CEF Personnel Files; Reference: RG 150; Volume: Box 292 - 24.
[Source citation includes one media item]

69   Ancestry.com, Ontario, Canada Births, 1869-1913 (Provo, UT, USA, Ancestry.com Operations Inc, 2010), Ancestry.com, Archives of Ontario; Series: MS929; Reel: 142.
[Source citation includes one media item]

70   Ancestry.com, Canada, Soldiers of the First World War, 1914-1918 (Provo, UT, USA, Ancestry.com Operations, Inc., 2006), Ancestry.com.
[Source citation includes one media item]

71   Ancestry.com, Ontario, Canada, Deaths, 1869-1938 and Deaths Overseas, 1939-1947 (Provo, UT, USA, Ancestry.com Operations Inc, 2010), Ancestry.com, Archives of Ontario; Toronto, Ontario, Canada; Collection: MS 935; Series: M023568; Reel: 683.
[Source citation includes one media item]

72   Ancestry.com, 1921 Census of Canada (Provo, UT, USA, Ancestry.com Operations Inc, 2013), Ancestry.com, Reference Number: RG 31; Folder Number: 56; Census Place: 56, Elgin West, Ontario; Page Number: 2.
[Source citation includes one media item]

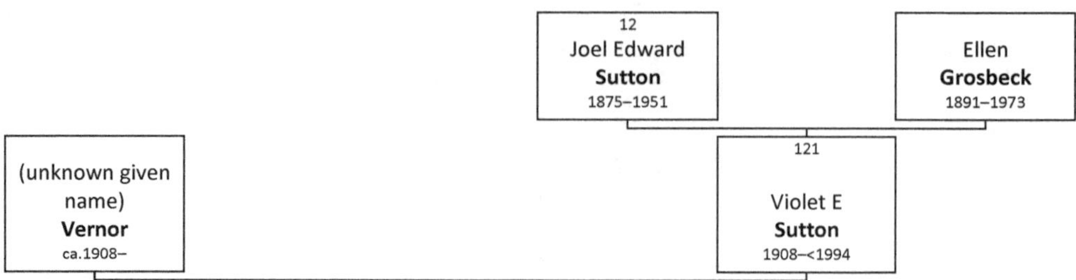

Here are the details about **Violet E Sutton's** second marriage with (unknown given name) Vernor. You can read more about Violet E on page 26.

(unknown given name) Vernor was born at (Likely) in Elgin, Ontario, Canada, about 1908.

Family of Edward Sutton and Evelyn Harp

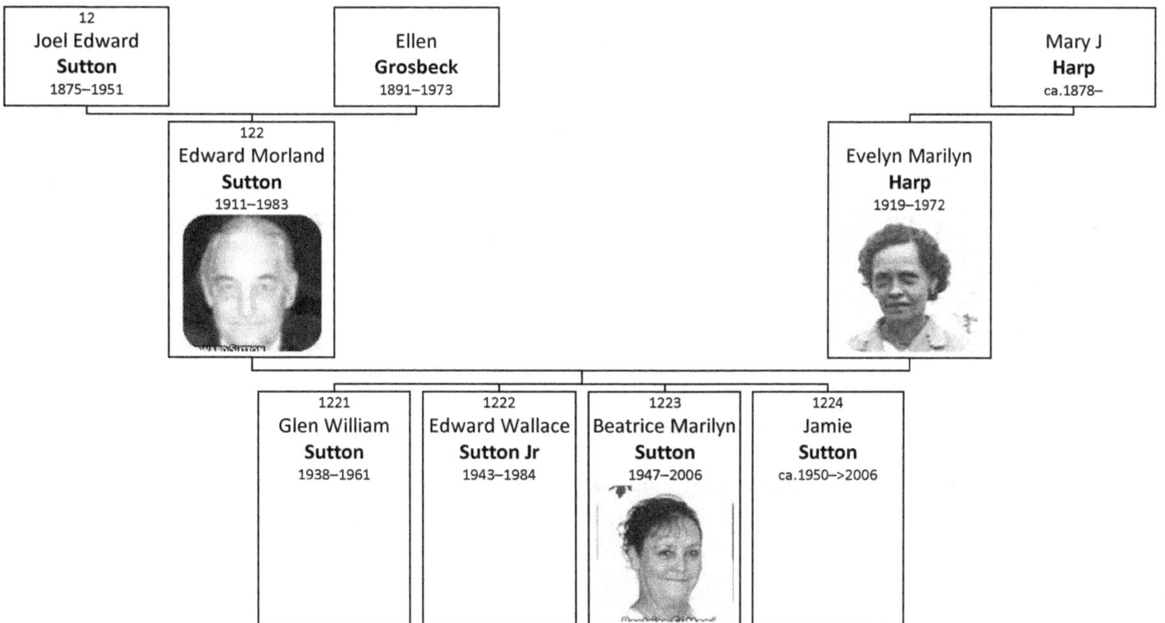

122. **Edward Morland[4] Sutton** was born on Tuesday, April 4, 1911, in Elgin, Ontario, Canada.[73–75] He was the son of Joel Edward Sutton (12) and Ellen Grosbeck.

Edward Morland died at Elgin General Hospital in St Thomas, Elgin, Ontario, Canada, on May 26, 1983, at the age of 72.

Edward Morland
Sutton

More facts and events for Edward Morland Sutton:

Residence:	1911	Elgin, Ontario, Canada[74]
		Single; Son / Cohab: Joel Sutton 38, Ellen Sutton 21, Violet Sutton 2, Edward Sutton 3m.
Residence:	June 1, 1921	Elgin, Ontario, Canada[73]
		Single; Son / Cohab: Joel Sutton 46, Ellen Sutton 30, Violet Sutton 13, Eddie Sutton 10, Andrew Sutton 8, Helen Sutton 6, Annie Sutton 4, E Lyin Sutton 2.
Residence:	1949	Elgin, Ontario, Canada[76]
		Cohab: Edward Dutton (Labourer); Mrs Edward Dutton

73   Ancestry.com, 1921 Census of Canada (Provo, UT, USA, Ancestry.com Operations Inc, 2013), Ancestry.com, Reference Number: RG 31; Folder Number: 56; Census Place: Dutton (Town), Elgin West, Ontario; Page Number: 8.
[Source citation includes one media item]

74   Ancestry.com, 1911 Census of Canada (Provo, UT, USA, Ancestry.com Operations Inc, 2006), Ancestry.com, Year: 1911; Census Place: 39 - Dutton, Elgin West, Ontario; Page: 17; Family No: 217.
[Source citation includes one media item]

75   Ancestry.com, Ontario, Canada Births, 1869-1913 (Provo, UT, USA, Ancestry.com Operations Inc, 2010), Ancestry.com, Archives of Ontario; Series: MS929; Reel: 218.
[Source citation includes one media item]

76   Ancestry.com, Canada, Voters Lists, 1935-1980 (Provo, UT, USA, Ancestry.com Operations, Inc., 2012), Ancestry.com, Library and Archives Canada; Ottawa, Ontario, Canada; Voters Lists, Federal Elections, 1935-1980.
[Source citation includes one media item]

Residence: 1957   Elgin, Ontario, Canada[76]
                             Cohab: Mrs Charlotte Sutton (widow); Andrew (Labourer); Mrs Andrew, Edward
                             (Labourer); Mrs Edward.
Residence: 1968   Elgin, Ontario, Canada[76]
                             Cohab: Edward Sutton (Labourer); Mrs Edward ; Junior Sutton (Labourer)

They had four children: Glen (1938–1961), Edward (1943–1984), Beatrice (1947–2006) and Jamie (ca.1950–>2006). Evelyn Marilyn Harp was born at Dutton in Elgin, Ontario, Canada, on Tuesday, April 15, 1919.[77] She was the daughter of Mary J Harp.

Evelyn Marilyn reached 53 years of age and died in St Thomas, Elgin, Ontario, Canada, on May 1, 1972.

Evelyn Marilyn Harp

More facts and events for Evelyn Marilyn Harp:

Residence: June 1, 1921   Elgin, Ontario, Canada[77]
                             Single; Dau / Cohab: Mary J Harp 43,   Norman Harp 11,   Lettie Harp 12,   Allice
                             Harp 5,   Evaline Harp 2.

[77]   Ancestry.com, 1921 Census of Canada (Provo, UT, USA, Ancestry.com Operations Inc, 2013), Ancestry.com, Reference Number: RG 31; Folder
       Number: 55; Census Place: Dunwich (Township), Elgin West, Ontario; Page Number: 18.
       [Source citation includes one media item]

Glen Sutton

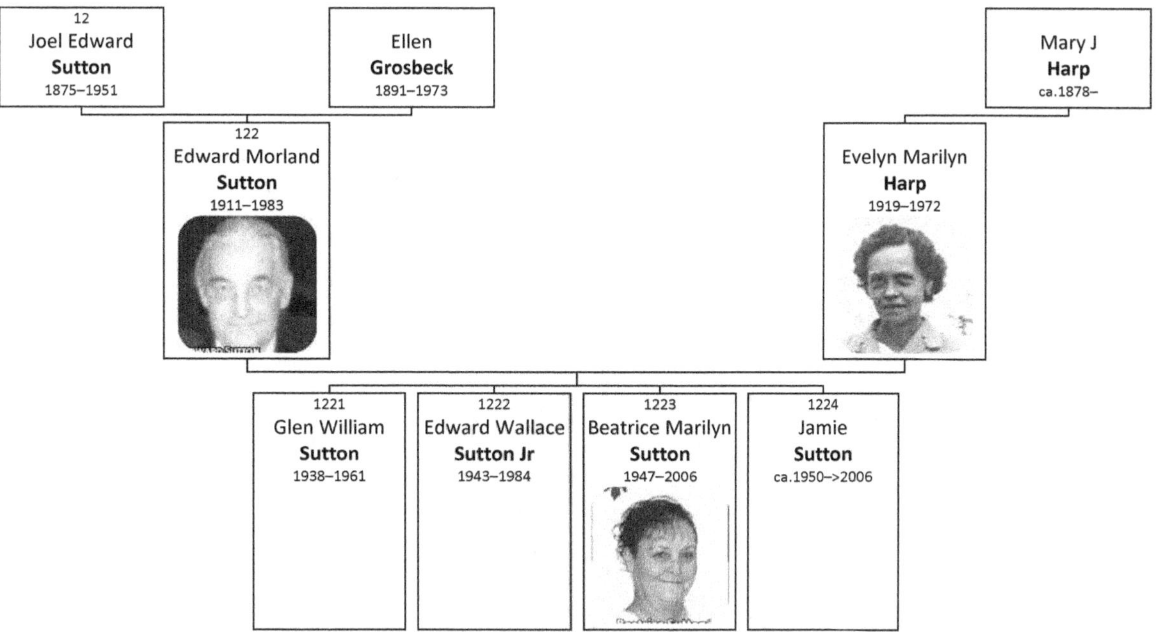

1221. **Glen William[5] Sutton** was born on Tuesday, December 27, 1938, at Dutton in Elgin, Ontario, Canada. He was the son of Edward Morland Sutton (122) and Evelyn Marilyn Harp. He was also known as **Pete Sutton**.

Glen William died at Dutton in Elgin, Ontario, Canada, on July 9, 1961, at the age of 22. He was buried at Dutton (Fairview Dutton Cemetery, Row 20, black granite #30) in Elgin, Ontario, Canada.

Figure 8: Fairview Cemetery - Dutton

Edward Sutton

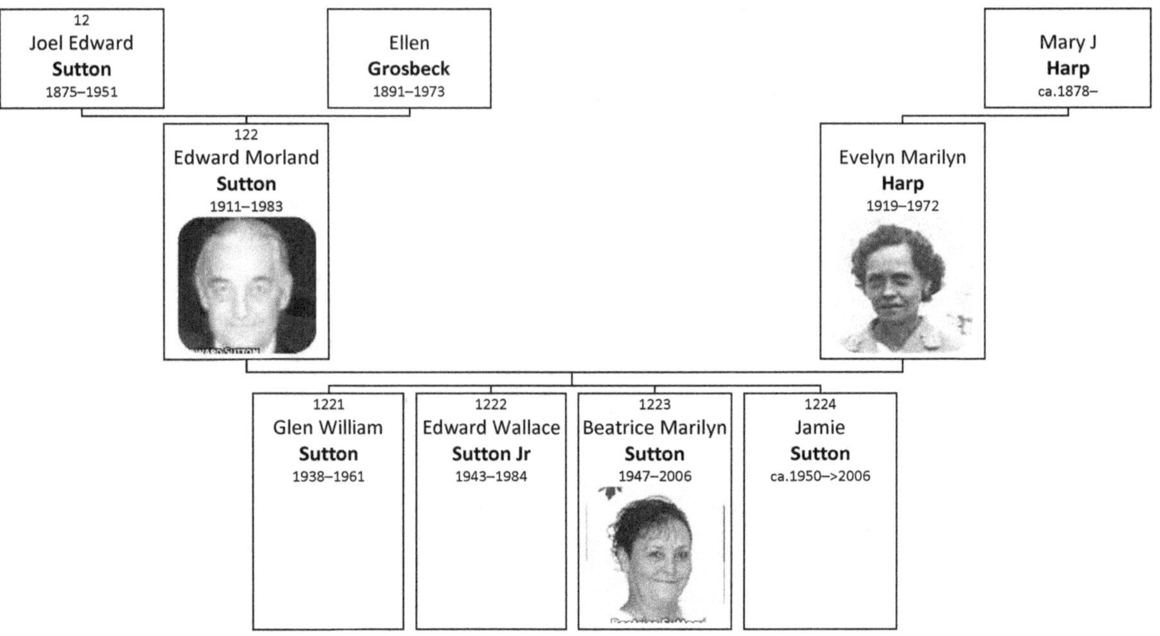

1222. **Edward Wallace[5] Sutton Jr** was born in 1943 at (Likely) in Elgin, Ontario, Canada. He was the son of Edward Morland Sutton (122) and Evelyn Marilyn Harp.

Edward Wallace died in Windsor, Essex, Ontario, Canada, in 1984 at the age of 41. He was buried at Dutton (Fairview Dutton Cemetery, Row 20 black granite #30) in Elgin, Ontario, Canada.

More facts and events for Edward Wallace Sutton Jr:

Residence: 1965   Elgin, Ontario, Canada[78]
            Cohab: Edward Sutton (labourer), Mrs Edward, Edward Junior (labourer)
Residence: 1972   Elgin, Ontario, Canada[78]
            Cohab: Edward M Leitch (retired); Edward W Leitch (Labourer)

More figures:
Page 31, Figure 8: Fairview Cemetery - Dutton

---

[78]   Ancestry.com, Canada, Voters Lists, 1935-1980 (Provo, UT, USA, Ancestry.com Operations, Inc., 2012), Ancestry.com, Library and Archives Canada; Ottawa, Ontario, Canada; Voters Lists, Federal Elections, 1935-1980.
[Source citation includes one media item]

Beatrice Sutton

1223. **Beatrice Marilyn[5] Sutton** was born on Wednesday, October 8, 1947, in St Thomas, Elgin, Ontario, Canada.[79, 80] She was the daughter of Edward Morland Sutton (122) and Evelyn Marilyn Harp.

Beatrice Marilyn died at University Hospital in London, Middlesex, Ontario, Canada, on July 18, 2006, at the age of 58.[79, 80] She was buried at Dutton (Fairview Cemetery) in Elgin, Ontario, Canada.

Beatrice Marilyn Sutton

More facts and events for Beatrice Marilyn Sutton:

Residence: 1958   London, Middlesex, Ontario, Canada[81]
           Cohab: Beatrice Sutton (Telephone Operator)
Residence: 1972   West Lorne, Elgin, Ontario, Canada[81]
           Cohab: Daniel McGill (Labourer), Mrs Beatrice McGill

Marriages with Daniel McGill and an unknown partner are known.

Figure 9: Fairview Dutton Cemetery

79   Ancestry.com, U.S. Cemetery and Funeral Home Collection (Provo, UT, USA, Ancestry.com Operations Inc, 2011), Ancestry.com, obitsforlife; Publication Place: Portland, Oregon, USA; URL: http://www.obitsforlife.com/obituary/277372/McGill-Bea-Beatrice.php.

80   Ancestry.com, Web: Obituary Daily Times Index, 1995-2012 (Provo, UT, USA, Ancestry.com Operations, Inc., 2012), Ancestry.com.

81   Ancestry.com, Canada, Voters Lists, 1935-1980 (Provo, UT, USA, Ancestry.com Operations, Inc., 2012), Ancestry.com, Library and Archives Canada; Ottawa, Ontario, Canada; Voters Lists, Federal Elections, 1935-1980.
      [Source citation includes one media item]

Family of Beatrice Sutton and Daniel McGill

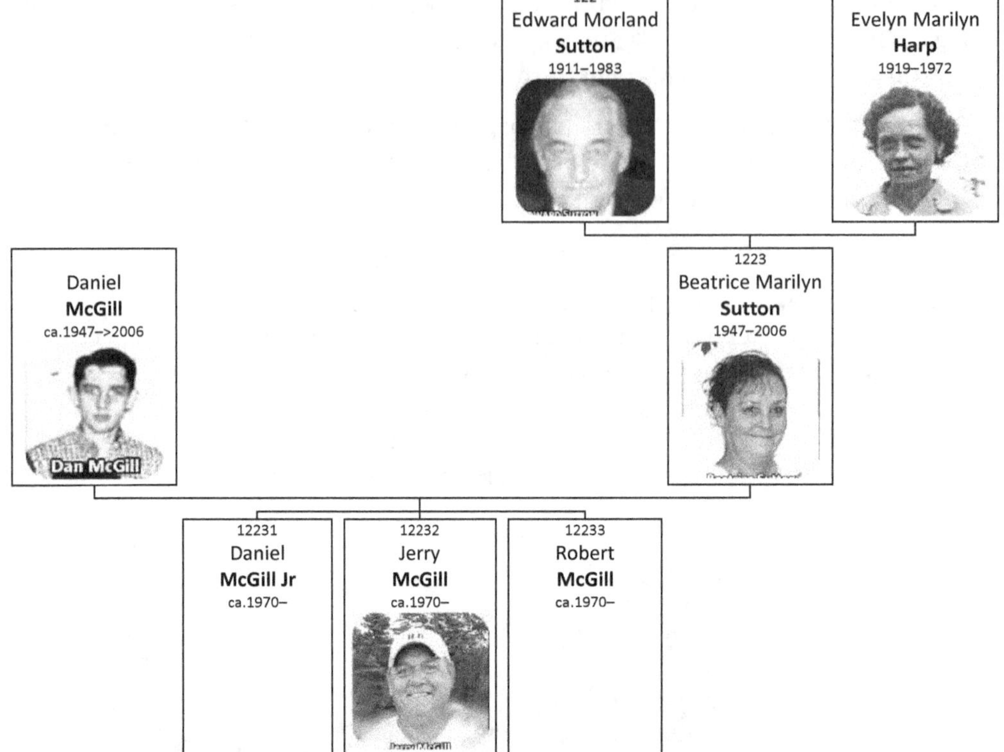

Here are the details about **Beatrice Marilyn Sutton's** first marriage with Daniel McGill. You can read more about Beatrice Marilyn on page 33.

They had three sons: Daniel (ca.1970–), Jerry (ca.1970–) and Robert (ca.1970–). Daniel McGill was born at (Likely) in Elgin, Ontario, Canada, about 1947.[82] He was also known as **Buck McGill**.

Daniel McGill

Daniel died at (Likely) in Elgin, Ontario, Canada, after 2006. "lovingly remembered" in wife's obituary.

More facts and events for Daniel McGill:

Residence: 1964   West Lorne, Elgin, Ontario, Canada[82]

Residence: 1972   West Lorne, Elgin, Ontario, Canada[81]
                    Cohab: Daniel McGill (Labourer), Mrs Beatrice McGill

Residence: 1974   West Lorne, Elgin, Ontario, Canada[81]

---

82   Ancestry.com, Canada, Selected School Yearbooks, 1908-2010 (Provo, UT, USA, Ancestry.com Operations, Inc., 2015), Ancestry.com, "Canada, Selected School Yearbooks, 1908-2010"; School: West Elgin High School; Year: 1964.
[Source citation includes one media item]

Family of Daniel McGill and Rose ()

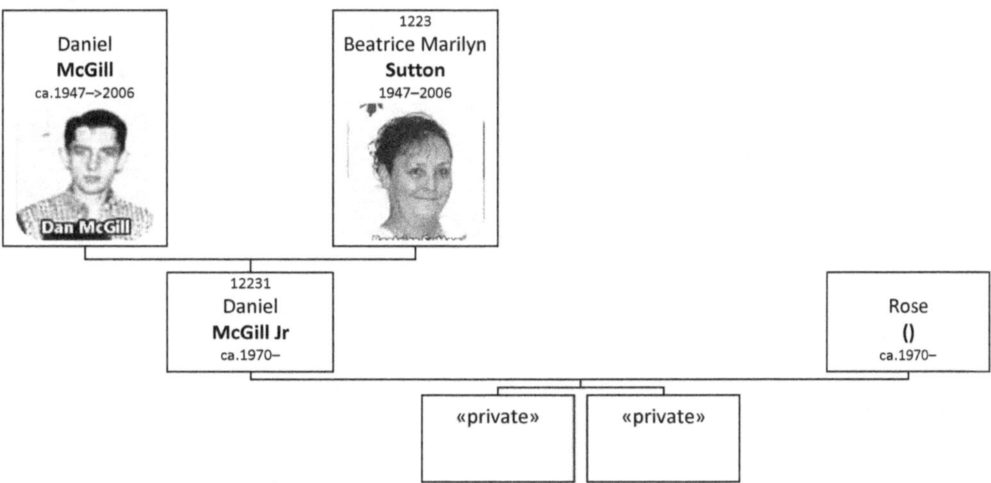

12231. **Daniel[6] McGill Jr** was born about 1970 at (Likely) in Elgin, Ontario, Canada. He is the son of Daniel McGill and Beatrice Marilyn Sutton (1223).

More facts and events for Daniel McGill Jr:

Residence: July 18, 2006   West Lorne, Elgin, Ontario, Canada
Residence cited in mother's obituary.

They have two children: «private» and «private». Rose () was born at (Likely) in Elgin, Ontario, Canada, about 1970.

Family of Jerry McGill and Chantell Wardle

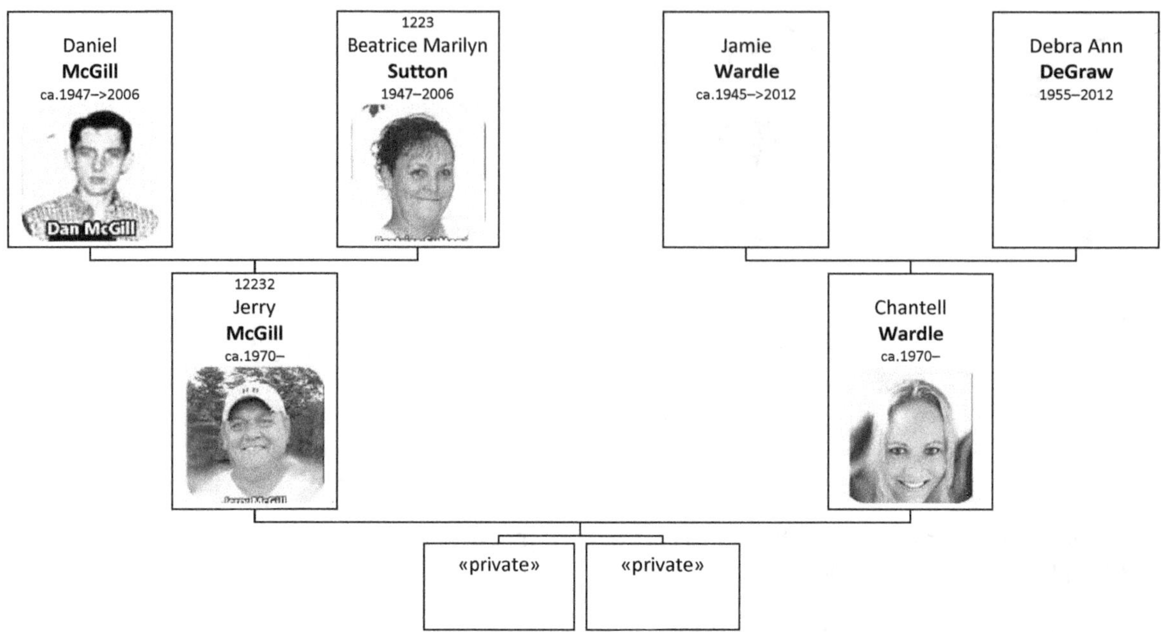

12232. **Jerry**[6] **McGill** was born about 1970 at (Likely) in Elgin, Ontario, Canada. He is the son of Daniel McGill and Beatrice Marilyn Sutton (1223).

Jerry McGill

More facts and events for Jerry McGill:

Residence: July 18, 2006   Rodney, Elgin, Ontario, Canada
Residence cited in mother's obituary.

They have two daughters: «private» and «private». Chantell Wardle was born at (Likely) in Rodney, Elgin, Ontario, Canada, about 1970. She is the daughter of Jamie Wardle and Debra Ann DeGraw.

Chantell Wardle

More facts and events for Chantell Wardle:

Residence: 2020   London, Middlesex, Ontario, Canada

Figure 10: Jerry and Chantell McGill
(September 6, 2020)

Family of Robert McGill and Susan ()

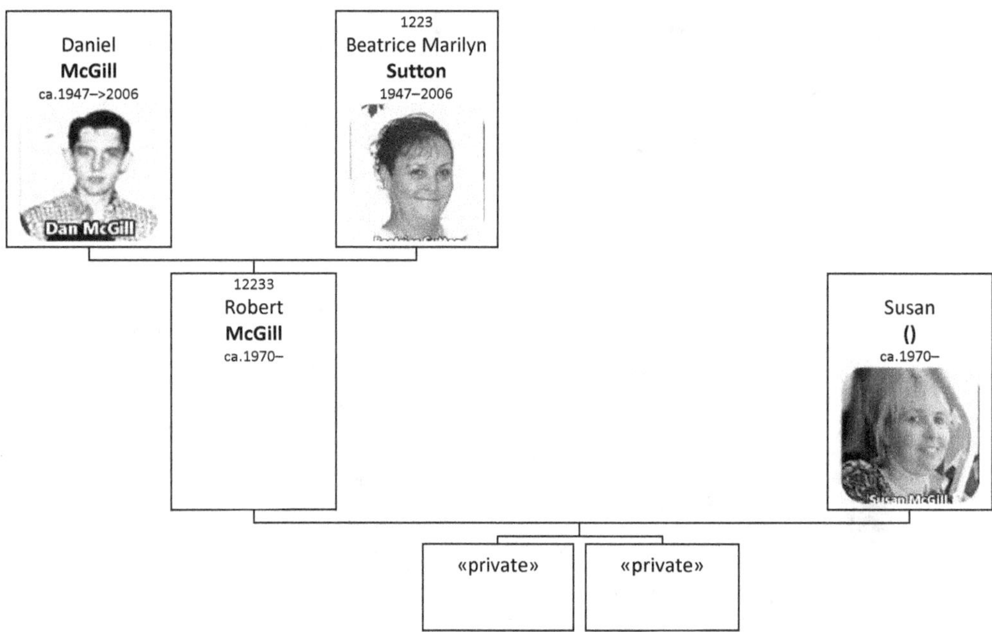

12233. **Robert**[6] **McGill** was born about 1970 at (Likely) in Elgin, Ontario, Canada. He is the son of Daniel McGill and Beatrice Marilyn Sutton (1223).

More facts and events for Robert McGill:

Residence: July 18, 2006   West Lorne, Elgin, Ontario, Canada
Residence cited in mother's obituary.

They have two daughters: «private» and «private». Susan () was born at (Likely) in Elgin, Ontario, Canada, about 1970.

Susan ()

More facts and events for Susan ():

Residence: Rodney, Elgin, Ontario, Canada[83]

---

83   Ancestry.com, Canadian Phone and Address Directories, 1995-2002 (Provo, UT, USA, Ancestry.com Operations Inc, 2005), Ancestry.com.

Beatrice Sutton

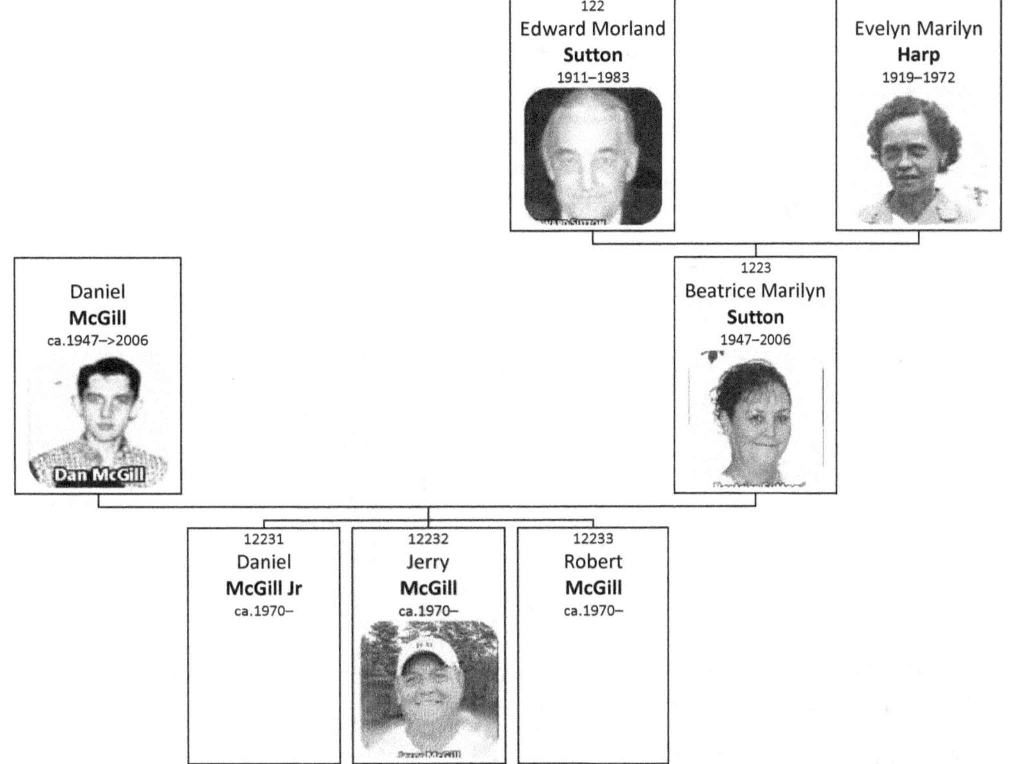

Here are the details about **Beatrice Marilyn Sutton's** second marriage with an unknown partner. You can read more about Beatrice Marilyn on page 33.

Jamie Sutton

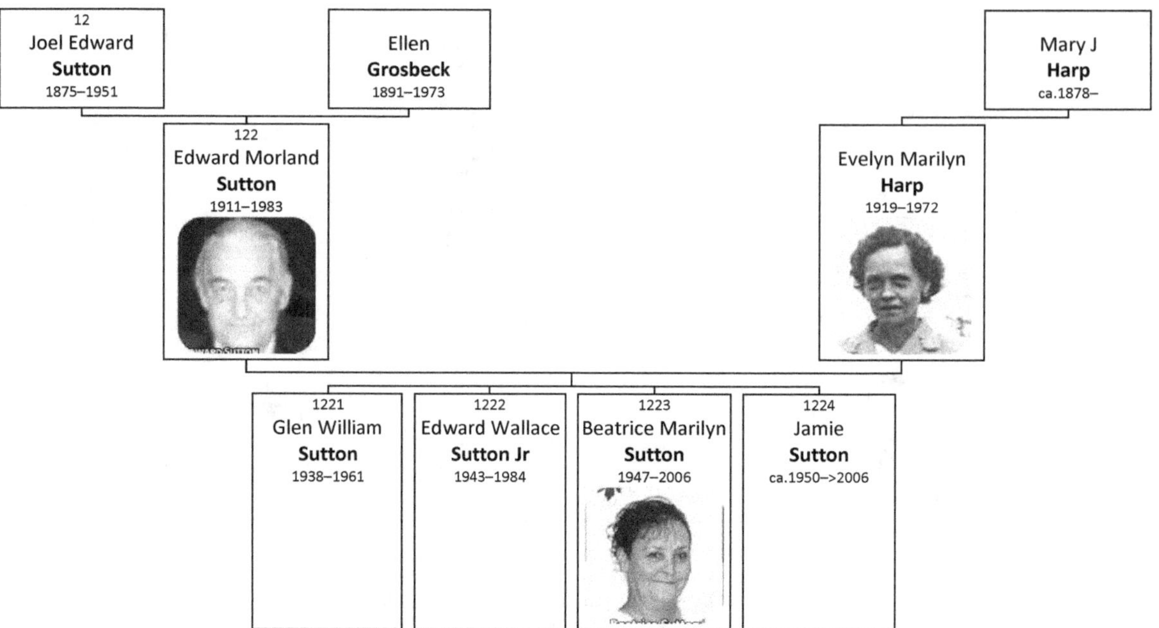

1224. **Jamie**[5] **Sutton** was born about 1950 at (Likely) in Elgin, Ontario, Canada. He was the son of Edward Morland Sutton (122) and Evelyn Marilyn Harp.

Jamie died after 2006. cited as living in sister Beatrice obituary.

More facts and events for Jamie Sutton:

Residence: July 18, 2006   London, Middlesex, Ontario, Canada
Residence cited in sister Beatrice obituary.

Andrew Sutton

123. **Andrew Robert[4] Sutton** was born on Monday, March 10, 1913, in St Thomas, Elgin, Ontario, Canada.[84, 85] He was the son of Joel Edward Sutton (12) and Ellen Grosbeck. He was also known as **Dick Sutton**.

Andrew Robert died in St Thomas, Elgin, Ontario, Canada, on November 7, 1993, at the age of 80.

More facts and events for Andrew Robert Sutton:

Residence: June 1, 1921   Elgin, Ontario, Canada[84]
Single;   Son / Cohab: Joel Sutton 46,   Ellen Sutton 30,   Violet Sutton 13, Eddie Sutton 10,   Andrew Sutton 8,   Helen Sutton 6,   Annie Sutton 4,   E Lyin Sutton 2.

Residence: 1957   Elgin, Ontario, Canada[86]
Cohab: Mrs Charlotte Sutton (widow), Andrew (labourer), Mrs Andrew, Edward (labourer), Mrs Edward

Residence: 1968   Elgin, Ontario, Canada[86]
Cohab: Andrew Sutton (labourer), Mrs Andrew

Marriages with Violet M Wilson and Lila Marie Haskett (Page 48) are known.

[84] Ancestry.com, 1921 Census of Canada (Provo, UT, USA, Ancestry.com Operations Inc, 2013), Ancestry.com, Reference Number: RG 31; Folder Number: 56; Census Place: Dutton (Town), Elgin West, Ontario; Page Number: 8.
[Source citation includes one media item]

[85] Ancestry.com, Ontario, Canada Births, 1869-1913 (Provo, UT, USA, Ancestry.com Operations Inc, 2010), Ancestry.com, Archives of Ontario; Series: MS929; Reel: 239.
[Source citation includes one media item]

[86] Ancestry.com, Canada, Voters Lists, 1935-1980 (Provo, UT, USA, Ancestry.com Operations, Inc., 2012), Ancestry.com, Library and Archives Canada; Ottawa, Ontario, Canada; Voters Lists, Federal Elections, 1935-1980.
[Source citation includes one media item]

Family of Andrew Sutton and Violet Wilson

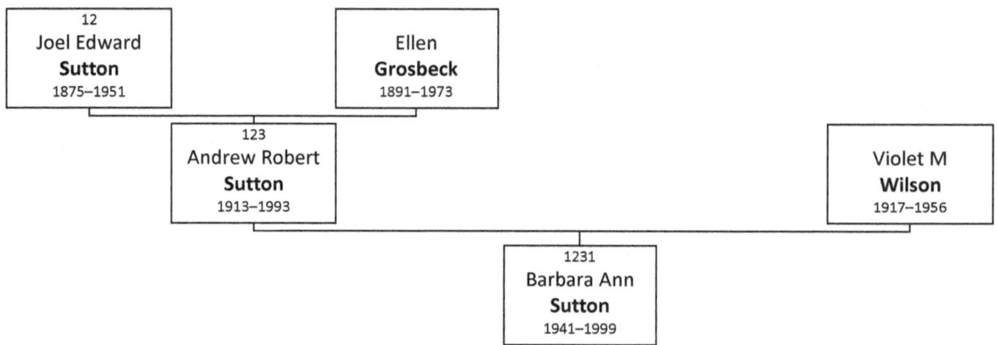

Here are the details about **Andrew Robert Sutton's** first marriage with Violet M Wilson. You can read more about Andrew Robert on page 41.

They had one daughter: Barbara (1941–1999). Violet M Wilson was born in St Thomas, Elgin, Ontario, Canada, in 1917.[87]

Violet M reached 39 years of age and died in 1956.[87] She was buried in St Thomas, Elgin, Ontario, Canada.[87]

87   Ancestry.com, Web: Canada, GenWeb Cemetery Index (Provo, UT, USA, Ancestry.com Operations, Inc., 2013), Ancestry.com.

Family of Barbara Sutton and Larry Hull

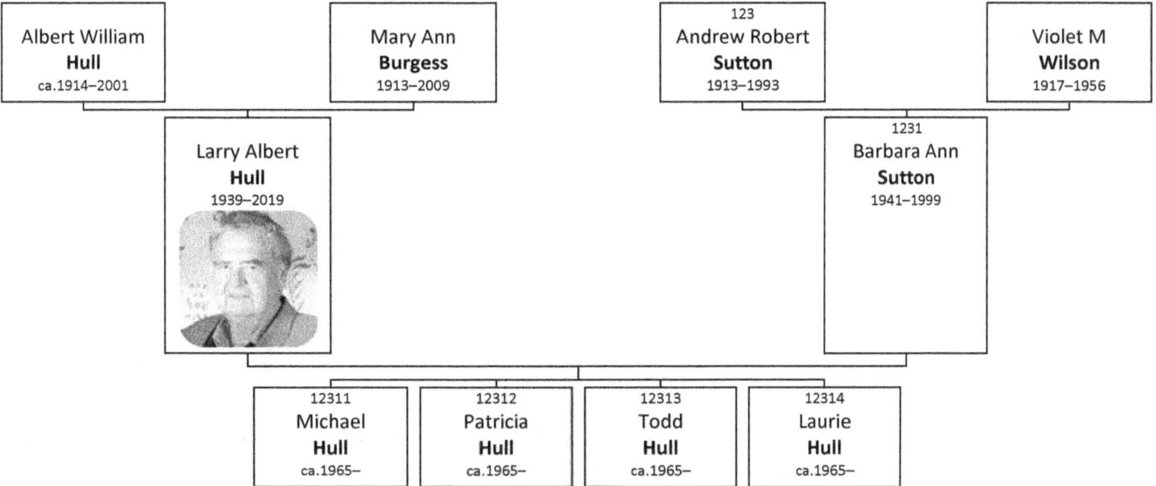

1231. **Barbara Ann[5] Sutton** was born on Monday, November 17, 1941, in St Thomas, Elgin, Ontario, Canada.[88] She was the daughter of Andrew Robert Sutton (123) and Violet M Wilson.

Barbara Ann died at Dutton in Elgin, Ontario, Canada, on July 20, 1999, at the age of 57.[88] She was buried at Dutton (Fairview Cemetery,   Dutton, Elgin County, Ontario, Canada,   PLOT: Row 3) in Elgin, Ontario, Canada.[88]

They had four children: Michael (ca.1965–), Patricia (ca.1965–), Todd (ca.1965–) and Laurie (ca.1965–). Larry Albert Hull was born at Dutton in Elgin, Ontario, Canada, on Wednesday, February 15, 1939.[88] He was the son of Albert William Hull and Mary Ann Burgess.

Larry Albert Hull

Larry Albert reached 80 years of age and died in St Thomas, Elgin, Ontario, Canada, on June 9, 2019.[88]

He was buried at Dutton (Fairview Cemetery,   Dutton, Elgin County, Ontario, Canada,   PLOT: Row 3) in Elgin, Ontario, Canada.[88]

More facts and events for Larry Albert Hull:

Residence: 1972   Elgin, Ontario, Canada[89]
             Cohab: Larry Hull (labourer); Mrs Larry Hull
Residence: 1974   Elgin, Ontario, Canada[89]
             Cohab: Larry A Hull (Dept Highways); Mrs Barbara Hull

More figures:
Page 33, Figure 9: Fairview Dutton Cemetery

---

88   Ancestry.com, Canada, Find A Grave Index, 1600s-Current (Provo, UT, USA, Ancestry.com Operations, Inc., 2012), Ancestry.com.

89   Ancestry.com, Canada, Voters Lists, 1935-1980 (Provo, UT, USA, Ancestry.com Operations, Inc., 2012), Ancestry.com, Library and Archives Canada; Ottawa, Ontario, Canada; Voters Lists, Federal Elections, 1935-1980.
      [Source citation includes one media item]

Family of Michael Hull and Susan ()

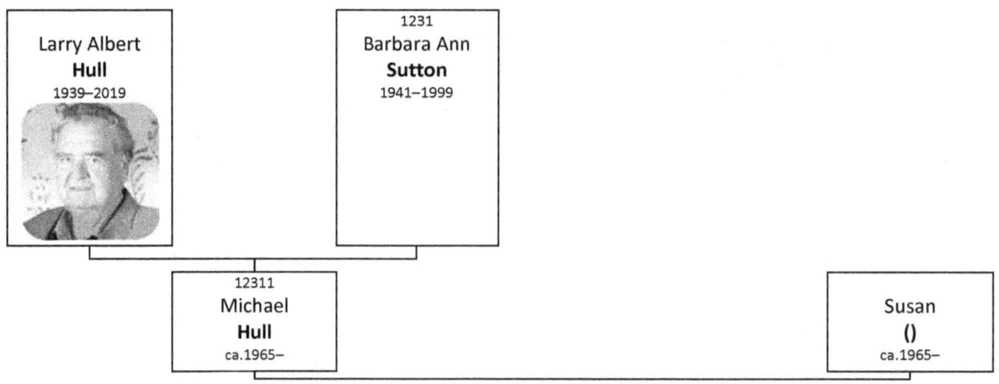

12311. Michael[6] Hull was born about 1965 at (Likely), Dutton in Elgin, Ontario, Canada. He is the son of Larry Albert Hull and Barbara Ann Sutton (1231).

Susan () was born at (Likely), Dutton in Elgin, Ontario, Canada, about 1965.

Family of Patricia Hull and John Van Vugt

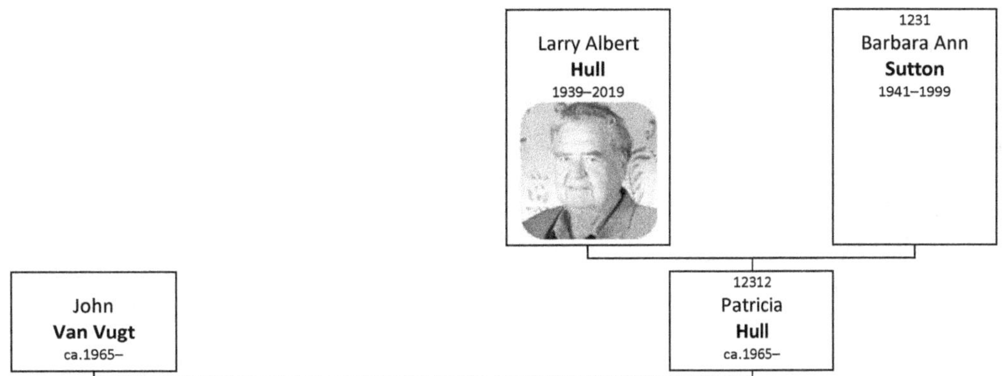

12312. **Patricia**[6] **Hull** was born about 1965 at (Likely), Dutton in Elgin, Ontario, Canada. She is the daughter of Larry Albert Hull and Barbara Ann Sutton (1231).

John Van Vugt was born at (Likely), Dutton in Elgin, Ontario, Canada, about 1965.

Family of Todd Hull and Noreen ()

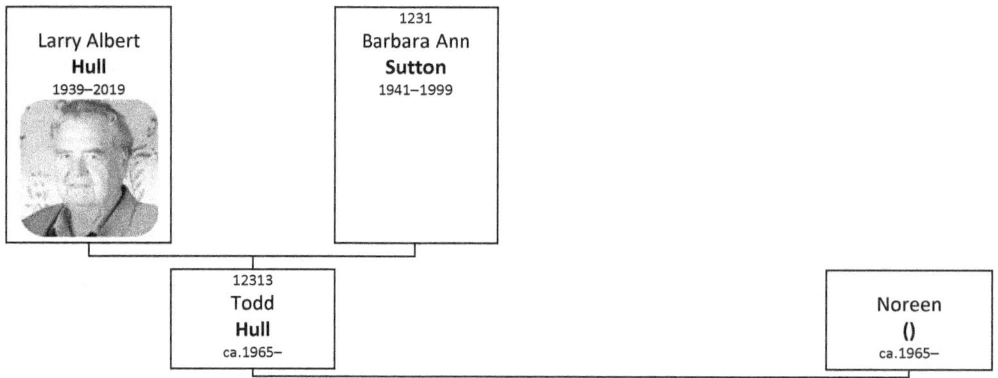

12313. **Todd**[6] **Hull** was born about 1965 at (Likely), Dutton in Elgin, Ontario, Canada. He is the son of Larry Albert Hull and Barbara Ann Sutton (1231).

Noreen () was born at (Likely), Dutton in Elgin, Ontario, Canada, about 1965.

Family of Laurie Hull and Ken Dawson

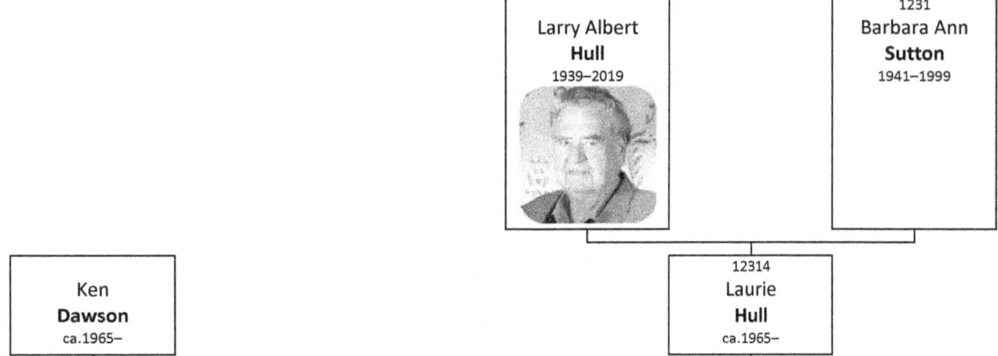

12314. Laurie[6] **Hull** was born about 1965 at (Likely), Dutton in Elgin, Ontario, Canada. She is the daughter of Larry Albert Hull and Barbara Ann Sutton (1231).

Ken Dawson was born at (Likely), Dutton in Elgin, Ontario, Canada, about 1965.

Family of Andrew Sutton and Lila Haskett

Here are the details about **Andrew Robert Sutton's** second marriage with Lila Marie Haskett. You can read more about Andrew Robert on page 41.

Lila Marie Haskett was born in St Thomas, Elgin, Ontario, Canada, on Monday, April 30, 1928. Lila Marie reached 88 years of age and died in St Thomas, Elgin, Ontario, Canada, on August 28, 2016. Her body was cremated at Dutton in Elgin, Ontario, Canada.

Family of Helen Sutton and Wesley Fennell

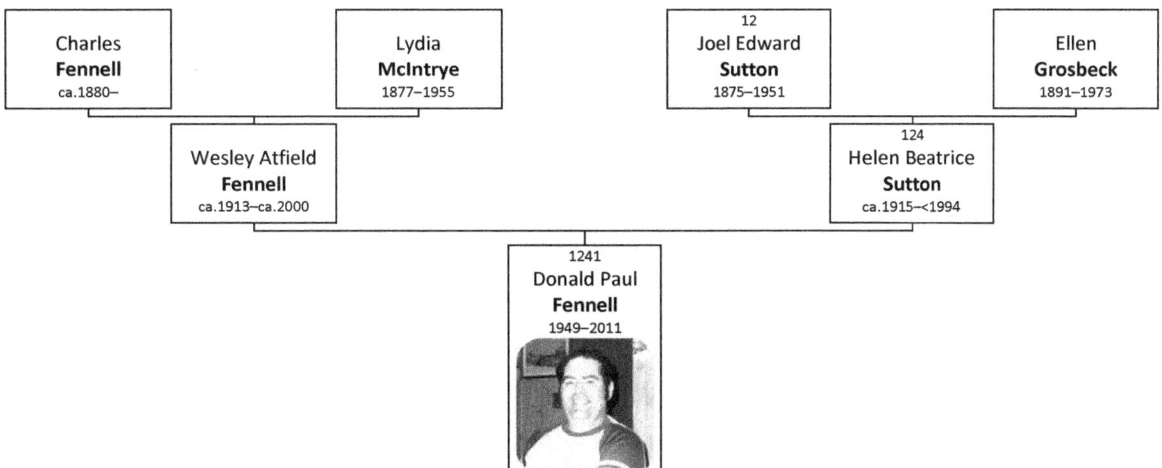

124. **Helen Beatrice[4] Sutton** was born about 1915 at Dutton in Elgin, Ontario, Canada.[90, 91] She was the daughter of Joel Edward Sutton (12) and Ellen Grosbeck.

Helen Beatrice died before 1994. Mentioned as deceased in mother's obituary.

More facts and events for Helen Beatrice Sutton:

Residence: June 1, 1921   Elgin, Ontario, Canada[90]
Single; Dau / Cohab: Joel Sutton 46,   Ellen Sutton 30,   Violet Sutton 13,   Eddie Sutton 10,   Andrew Sutton 8,   Helen Sutton 6,   Annie Sutton 4,   E Lyin Sutton 2.

Residence: 1972   St Thomas, Elgin, Ontario, Canada[92]
Cohab: Wesley Fennell (Tool & Die), Helen (RNA), Donald (labourer)

They had one son: Donald (1949–2011). Wesley Atfield Fennell was born at Newbury in Middlesex, Ontario, Canada, about 1913.[91, 93, 94] He was the son of Charles Fennell and Lydia McIntrye. They were his parents by adoption.

Wesley Atfield reached 87 years of age and died in Grand Bend, Huron, Ontario, Canada, about 2000.[93]

90   Ancestry.com, 1921 Census of Canada (Provo, UT, USA, Ancestry.com Operations Inc, 2013), Ancestry.com, Reference Number: RG 31; Folder Number: 56; Census Place: Dutton (Town), Elgin West, Ontario; Page Number: 8.
[Source citation includes one media item]

91   Ancestry.com and Genealogical Research Library (Brampton, Ontario, Canada), Ontario, Canada, Marriages, 1801-1928 (Provo, UT, USA, Ancestry.com Operations, Inc., 2010), Ancestry.com, Archives of Ontario; Toronto, Ontario, Canada; Registration of Marriages 1936; Reel: 10-999.
[Source citation includes one media item]

92   Ancestry.com, Canada, Voters Lists, 1935-1980 (Provo, UT, USA, Ancestry.com Operations, Inc., 2012), Ancestry.com, Library and Archives Canada; Ottawa, Ontario, Canada; Voters Lists, Federal Elections, 1935-1980.
[Source citation includes one media item]

93   Ancestry.com, Web: Obituary Daily Times Index, 1995-2012 (Provo, UT, USA, Ancestry.com Operations, Inc., 2012), Ancestry.com.

94   Ancestry.com, 1921 Census of Canada (Provo, UT, USA, Ancestry.com Operations Inc, 2013), Ancestry.com, Reference Number: RG 31; Folder Number: 72; Census Place: 72, Middlesex West, Ontario; Page Number: 1.
[Source citation includes one media item]

More facts and events for Wesley Atfield Fennell:

Residence: June 1, 1921   Middlesex, Ontario, Canada[94]
                             Anglican; Single;   Adopted Child / Cohab: Eharlie Fennell 47,   Mary Jane Fennell
                             45,   Lgdia Fennell 43,   Wisley Atfield Fennell 6.
Residence: 1965   St Thomas, Elgin, Ontario, Canada[92]
                             Cohab: Wesley Fennell (machinst); Mrs Wesley
Residence: 1972   St Thomas, Elgin, Ontario, Canada[92]
                             Cohab: Wesley Fennell (Tool & Die), Helen (RNA), Donald (labourer)

Family of Donald Fennell and Linda Merritt

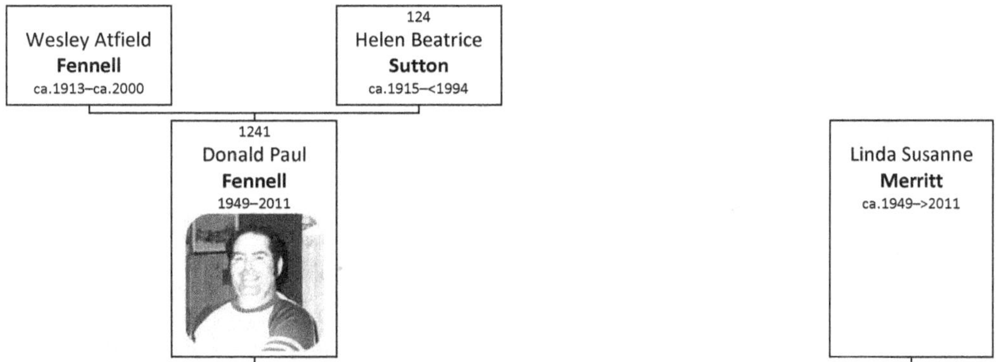

1241. **Donald Paul**[5] **Fennell** was born on Sunday, February 20, 1949, at Aldborough in Elgin, Ontario, Canada.[95] He was the son of Wesley Atfield Fennell and Helen Beatrice Sutton (124).

Donald Paul Fennell

Donald Paul died at Victoria Hospital, Critical Care Trauma Unit, London Ontario in London, Middlesex, Ontario, Canada, on March 31, 2011, at the age of 62.[95]

He was buried at Elmdale Memorial Park Cemetery,   St. Thomas, Elgin County, Ontario, Canada in St Thomas, Elgin, Ontario, Canada.[95]

More facts and events for Donald Paul Fennell:

Residence: 1972   St Thomas, Elgin, Ontario, Canada[96]
                       Cohab: Wesley Fennell (Tool & Die), Helen (RNA), Donald (labourer)
Residence: 1996 - 2002   St Thomas, Elgin, Ontario, Canada[97]

Linda Susanne Merritt was born at (Likely) in Elgin, Ontario, Canada, about 1949. Linda Susanne died after 2011.

95 Ancestry.com, Canada, Find A Grave Index, 1600s-Current (Provo, UT, USA, Ancestry.com Operations, Inc., 2012), Ancestry.com.

96 Ancestry.com, Canada, Voters Lists, 1935-1980 (Provo, UT, USA, Ancestry.com Operations, Inc., 2012), Ancestry.com, Library and Archives Canada; Ottawa, Ontario, Canada; Voters Lists, Federal Elections, 1935-1980.
    [Source citation includes one media item]

97 Ancestry.com, Canadian Phone and Address Directories, 1995-2002 (Provo, UT, USA, Ancestry.com Operations Inc, 2005), Ancestry.com.

Figure 11: Elmdale Memorial Park Cemetery

Family of Ann Sutton and Wilfred Snelgrove

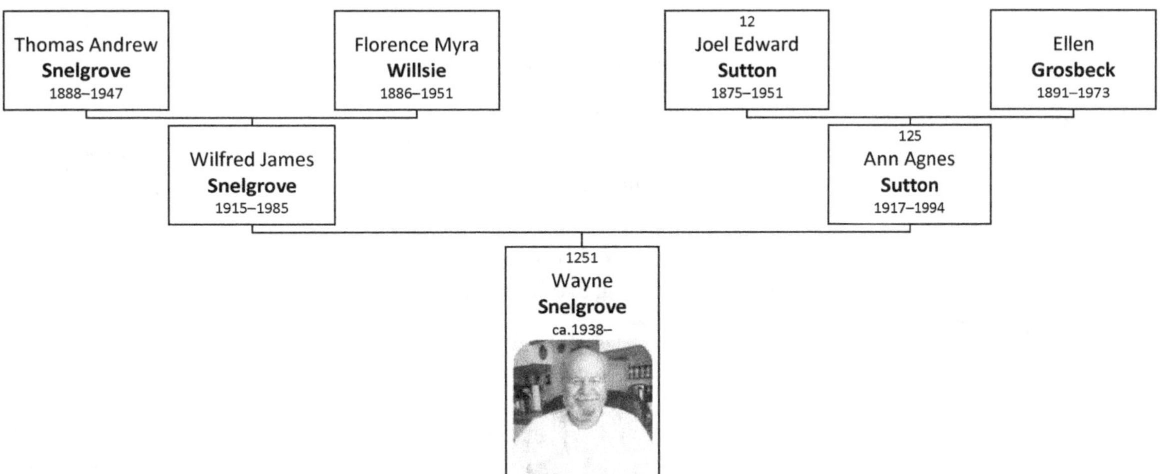

125. **Ann Agnes[4] Sutton** was born on Monday, October 15, 1917, at Dutton in Elgin, Ontario, Canada.[98–103] She was the daughter of Joel Edward Sutton (12) and Ellen Grosbeck.

Ann Agnes died at Caressant Care Nursing Home and ded in St Thomas Elgin General Hospital in St Thomas, Elgin, Ontario, Canada, on April 11, 1994, at the age of 76.[99, 101, 103] She was buried at Cremation: Funeral services at Arn Funeral Home, Dutton in St Thomas, Elgin, Ontario, Canada, on April 13, 1994.[103]

More facts and events for Ann Agnes Sutton:

Residence: June 1, 1921   Elgin, Ontario, Canada[98]
Single; Dau / Cohab: Joel Sutton 46,   Ellen Sutton 30,   Violet Sutton 13,   Eddie Sutton 10,   Andrew Sutton 8,   Helen Sutton 6,   Annie Sutton 4,   E Lyin Sutton 2.

Residence: 1959   Sutherlin, Douglas, Oregon, USA[102]

They had one son: Wayne (ca.1938–). Wilfred James Snelgrove was born at Caradoc in Middlesex, Ontario, Canada, on Sunday, August 29, 1915.[100, 101, 104, 105] He was the son of Thomas Andrew Snelgrove and Florence Myra Willsie. He was also known as **Jim Snelgrove**.

---

[98] Ancestry.com, 1921 Census of Canada (Provo, UT, USA, Ancestry.com Operations Inc, 2013), Ancestry.com, Reference Number: RG 31; Folder Number: 56; Census Place: Dutton (Town), Elgin West, Ontario; Page Number: 8.
[Source citation includes one media item]

[99] Ancestry.com, U.S., Social Security Applications and Claims Index, 1936-2007 (Provo, UT, USA, Ancestry.com Operations, Inc., 2015), Ancestry.com.

[100] Ancestry.com and Genealogical Research Library (Brampton, Ontario, Canada), Ontario, Canada, Marriages, 1801-1928 (Provo, UT, USA, Ancestry.com Operations, Inc., 2010), Ancestry.com, Archives of Ontario; Toronto, Ontario, Canada; Registration of Marriages 1936; Reel: 10-666.
[Source citation includes one media item]

[101] Ancestry.com, U.S., Social Security Death Index, 1935-Current (Provo, UT, USA, Ancestry.com Operations Inc, 2011), Ancestry.com, Social Security Administration; Washington D.C., USA; Social Security Death Index, Master File.

[102] Ancestry.com, U.S. Public Records Index, Volume 2 (Provo, UT, USA, Ancestry.com Operations, Inc., 2010), Ancestry.com.

[103] Ancestry.com, Beta: Newspapers.com Obituary Index, 1940-1955 (Lehi, UT, USA, Ancestry.com Operations Inc, 2019), Ancestry.com, The Windsor Star; Publication Date: 12/ Apr/ 1994; Publication Place: Windsor, Ontario, Canada; URL: https://www.newspapers.com/image/504195986/?article=52c807a2-5579-4900-80fa-c9c59fed793a&focus=0.3402803,0.55137527,0.4435393 8,0.7366729&xid=2378.

Wilfred James reached 69 years of age and died in Sutherlin, Douglas, Oregon, USA, on May 5, 1985.[101, 105]

More facts and events for Wilfred James Snelgrove:

Residence: June 1, 1921 Middlesex, Ontario, Canada[104]
Presbyterian;   Single;   Son / Cohab: Thomas Snelgrove 33,   Florence Snelgrove 26,   Melvine Snelgrove 13,   Wilma Snelgrove 11,   Francis Snelgrove 9, Wilfred Snelgrove 5,   Earnest Snelgrove 1.

Residence: 1940 Strathroy, Middlesex, Ontario, Canada[106]
Cohab: Wilfred Snelgrove (Labourer); Mrs Wilfred

Residence: 1957 California, USA[101]

Figure 12: Wilfred and Annie Snelgrove

Figure 13: Obituary for Annie SNELGROVE-at (Aged 77) (April 12, 1994)

---

[104] Ancestry.com, 1921 Census of Canada (Provo, UT, USA, Ancestry.com Operations Inc, 2013), Ancestry.com, Reference Number: RG 31; Folder Number: 72; Census Place: 72, Middlesex West, Ontario; Page Number: 3.
[Source citation includes one media item]

[105] Ancestry.com, Oregon, Death Index, 1898-2008 (Provo, UT, USA, Ancestry.com Operations Inc, 2000), Ancestry.com, Oregon State Library; 1966-1970 Death Index; Reel Title: State of Oregon Death Index; Year Range: 1981-1990.
[Source citation includes one media item]

[106] Ancestry.com, Canada, Voters Lists, 1935-1980 (Provo, UT, USA, Ancestry.com Operations, Inc., 2012), Ancestry.com, Library and Archives Canada; Ottawa, Ontario, Canada; Voters Lists, Federal Elections, 1935-1980.
[Source citation includes one media item]

Family of Wayne Snelgrove and Helen Dumeah

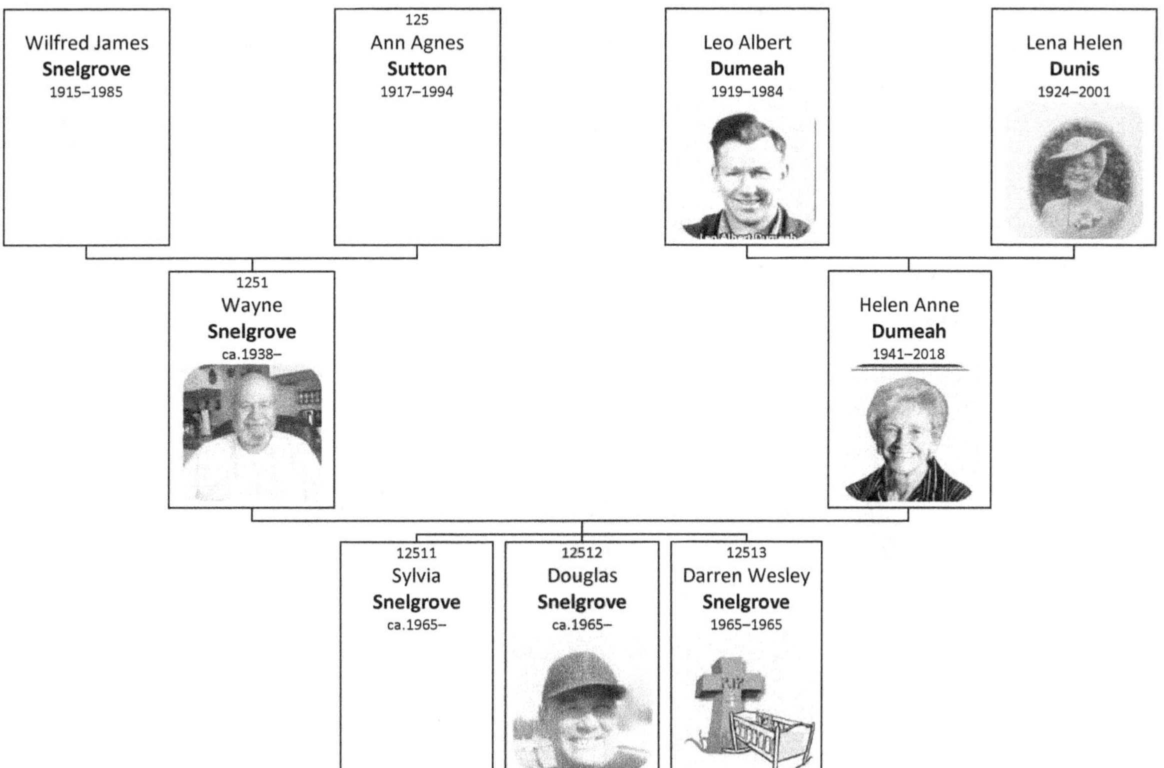

1251. **Wayne**[5] **Snelgrove** was born about 1938 at (Likely) in St Thomas, Elgin, Ontario, Canada. He is the son of Wilfred James Snelgrove and Ann Agnes Sutton (125).

Wayne Snelgrove

More facts and events for Wayne Snelgrove:

Residence:	1962	London, Middlesex, Ontario, Canada[107]
		Occupation : doorman
Residence:	1972	Chatham-Kent, Kent, Ontario, Canada[107]
		Cohab: Wayne Snelgrove (labourer); Mrs Kathy
Residence:	1974	Windsor, Essex, Ontario, Canada[107]
		Cohab: Wayne Snelgrove (assembler); Mrs Helen
Residence:	1995 - 2002	Windsor, Essex, Ontario, Canada[108]

---

107   Ancestry.com, Canada, Voters Lists, 1935-1980 (Provo, UT, USA, Ancestry.com Operations, Inc., 2012), Ancestry.com, Library and Archives Canada; Ottawa, Ontario, Canada; Voters Lists, Federal Elections, 1935-1980.
[Source citation includes one media item]

108   Ancestry.com, Canadian Phone and Address Directories, 1995-2002 (Provo, UT, USA, Ancestry.com Operations Inc, 2005), Ancestry.com.

They had three children: Sylvia (ca.1965–), Douglas (ca.1965–) and Darren (1965–1965). Helen Anne Dumeah was born in Windsor, Essex, Ontario, Canada, on Monday, December 15, 1941.[109, 110] She was the daughter of Leo Albert Dumeah and Lena Helen Dunis.

Helen Anne Dumeah

Helen Anne reached 76 years of age and died in Windsor, Essex, Ontario, Canada, on July 1, 2018.[109, 110]

She was buried at Heavenly Rest Cemetery in Windsor, Essex, Ontario, Canada.

More facts and events for Helen Anne Dumeah:

Residence: April 18, 1984   Windsor, Essex, Ontario, Canada
Residence cited in father's obituary.

Figure 14: Helen and Wayne Snelgrove
(2017)
abt 1 year before Helen died

---

[109] Ancestry.com, Canada Obituary Collection (Provo, UT, USA, Ancestry.com Operations Inc, 2006), Ancestry.com, Windsor Star; Publication Place: Windsor, On, Can; URL: http://www.legacy.com/obituaries/windsorstar/obituary.aspx?n=helen-snelgrove&pid=189450839.

[110] Ancestry.com, Beta: Newspapers.com Obituary Index, 1940-1955 (Lehi, UT, USA, Ancestry.com Operations Inc, 2019), Ancestry.com, The Windsor Star; Publication Date: 3/ Jul/ 2018; Publication Place: Windsor, Ontario, Canada; URL: https://www.newspapers.com/image/488141054/?article=2c872620-1e72-441d-96f3-f969a93b3a72&focus=0.5826073,0.33055583,0.7625733,0.5478035&xid=2378.

Family of Sylvia Snelgrove and John Colagiacomo

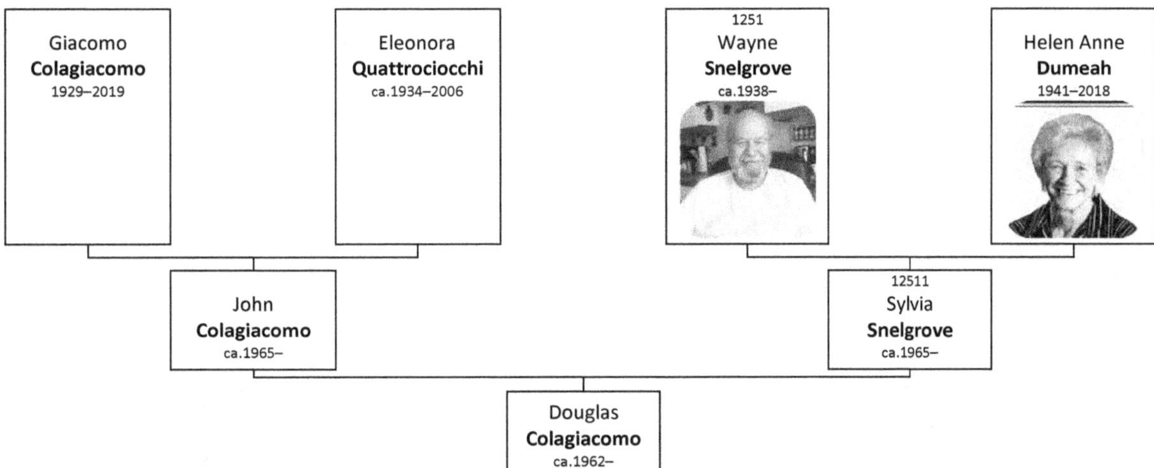

12511. **Sylvia**[6] **Snelgrove** was born about 1965 at (Likely) in Windsor, Essex, Ontario, Canada. She is the daughter of Wayne Snelgrove (1251) and Helen Anne Dumeah.

They have one son: Douglas (ca.1962–). John Colagiacomo was born at (Likely) in Essex, Ontario, Canada, about 1965. He is the son of Giacomo Colagiacomo and Eleonora Quattrociocchi.

More facts and events for John Colagiacomo:

Residence: 1995 - 2002   Windsor, Essex, Ontario, Canada[111]

111   Ancestry.com, Canadian Phone and Address Directories, 1995-2002 (Provo, UT, USA, Ancestry.com Operations Inc, 2005), Ancestry.com.

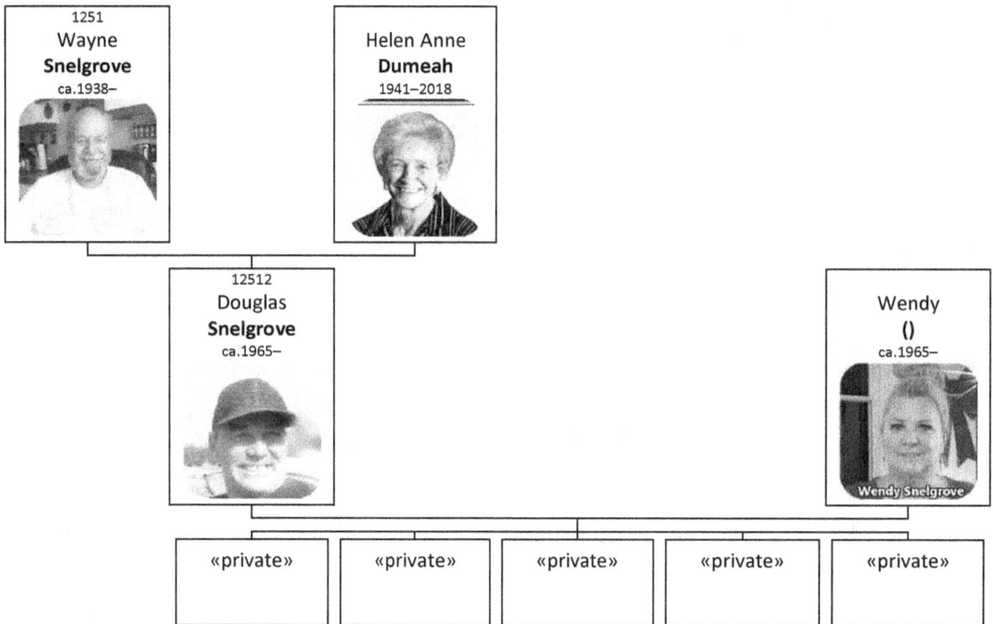

12512. **Douglas**[6] **Snelgrove** was born about 1965 at (Likely) in London, Middlesex, Ontario, Canada. He is the son of Wayne Snelgrove (1251) and Helen Anne Dumeah.

Douglas Snelgrove

They have five children: «private», «private», «private», «private» and «private». Wendy () was born at (Likely) in Windsor, Essex, Ontario, Canada, about 1965.

Wendy ()

Darren Snelgrove

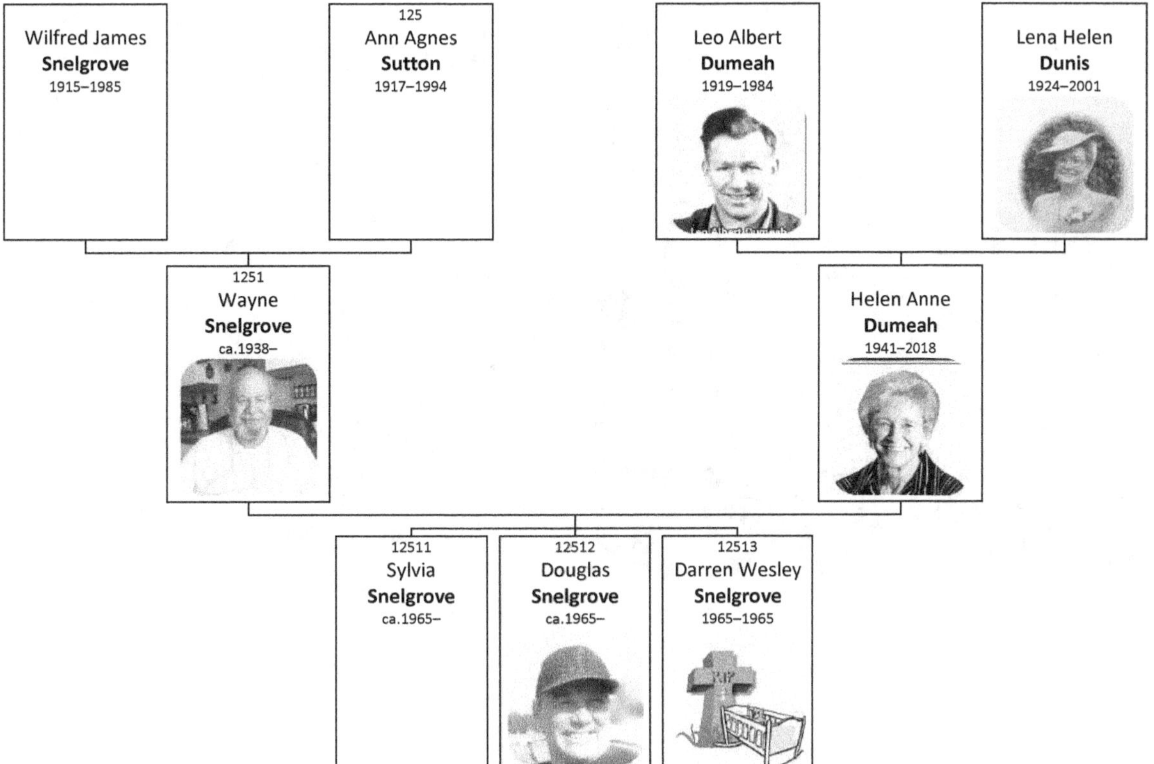

12513. **Darren Wesley**[6] **Snelgrove** was born on Wednesday, June 9, 1965, in Windsor, Essex, Ontario, Canada.[112, 113] He was the son of Wayne Snelgrove (1251) and Helen Anne Dumeah.

Darren Wesley died in Windsor, Essex, Ontario, Canada, on June 13, 1965.[112, 113] He was buried at Assumption Cemetery,　Windsor, Essex County, Ontario, Canada,　PLOT: Sec. E/Row 1/Stone #4 in Windsor, Essex, Ontario, Canada.[112, 113]

Darren Wesley
Snelgrove

112　Ancestry.com, U.S., Find A Grave Index, 1700s-Current (Provo, UT, USA, Ancestry.com Operations, Inc., 2012), Ancestry.com.

113　Ancestry.com, Canada, Find A Grave Index, 1600s-Current (Provo, UT, USA, Ancestry.com Operations, Inc., 2012), Ancestry.com.

Figure 15: Assumption Cemetery

Figure 16: Darren Wesley Snelgrove

Family of Elgin Sutton and Patricia Thompson

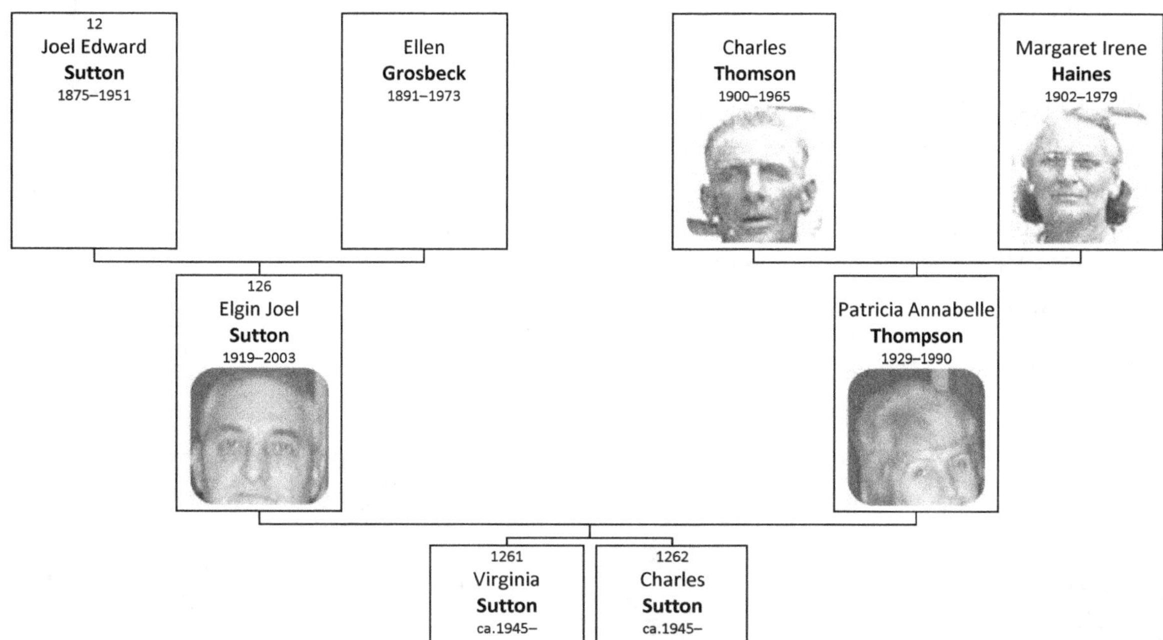

126. **Elgin Joel[4] Sutton** was born on Wednesday, December 17, 1919, at Dutton in Elgin, Ontario, Canada.[114–116] He was the son of Joel Edward Sutton (12) and Ellen Grosbeck.

Elgin Joel served in the military at Fought in WW2 in Europe between 1940 and 1945. He died in London, Middlesex, Ontario, Canada, in May 2003 at the age of 83.[115, 116] Elgin Joel was buried at Woodland Cemetery,   London   Middlesex County   Ontario, Canada in London, Middlesex, Ontario, Canada.[115]

Elgin Joel Sutton

More facts and events for Elgin Joel Sutton:

Residence:	June 1, 1921	Elgin, Ontario, Canada[114]
		Single; Son / Cohab: Joel Sutton 46, Ellen Sutton 30, Violet Sutton 13, Eddie Sutton 10, Andrew Sutton 8, Helen Sutton 6, Annie Sutton 4, E Lyin Sutton 2.
Residence:	1958	London, Middlesex, Ontario, Canada[117]
		Cohab: Elgin Sutton (city employee); Mrs Elgin
Residence:	April 11, 1994	London, Middlesex, Ontario, Canada
		Residence cited in mother's obituary.
Residence:		London, Middlesex, Ontario, Canada[118]

114   Ancestry.com, 1921 Census of Canada (Provo, UT, USA, Ancestry.com Operations Inc, 2013), Ancestry.com, Reference Number: RG 31; Folder Number: 56; Census Place: Dutton (Town), Elgin West, Ontario; Page Number: 8.
[Source citation includes one media item]

115   Ancestry.com, Canada, Find A Grave Index, 1600s-Current (Provo, UT, USA, Ancestry.com Operations, Inc., 2012), Ancestry.com.

116   Ancestry.com, Web: Obituary Daily Times Index, 1995-2012 (Provo, UT, USA, Ancestry.com Operations, Inc., 2012), Ancestry.com.

117   Ancestry.com, Canada, Voters Lists, 1935-1980 (Provo, UT, USA, Ancestry.com Operations, Inc., 2012), Ancestry.com, Library and Archives Canada; Ottawa, Ontario, Canada; Voters Lists, Federal Elections, 1935-1980.
[Source citation includes one media item]

118   Ancestry.com, Canadian Phone and Address Directories, 1995-2002 (Provo, UT, USA, Ancestry.com Operations Inc, 2005), Ancestry.com.

They had two children: Virginia (ca.1945–) and Charles (ca.1945–). Patricia Annabelle Thompson was born in Ontario, Canada, on Sunday, July 28, 1929.[115] She was the daughter of Charles Thomson and Margaret Irene Haines.

Patricia Annabelle
Thompson

Patricia Annabelle reached 60 years of age and died at Died from cancer in London, Middlesex, Ontario, Canada, on April 14, 1990.[115]

She was buried at Woodland Cemetery,   London   Middlesex County   Ontario, Canada in London, Middlesex, Ontario, Canada.[115]

More facts and events for Patricia Annabelle Thompson:

Residence: 1965   London, Middlesex, Ontario, Canada[117]

Figure 17: Elgin & Pat(Thomson) Sutton

Figure 18: Elgin Sutton

Figure 19: Woodland Cemetery - London

Virginia Sutton

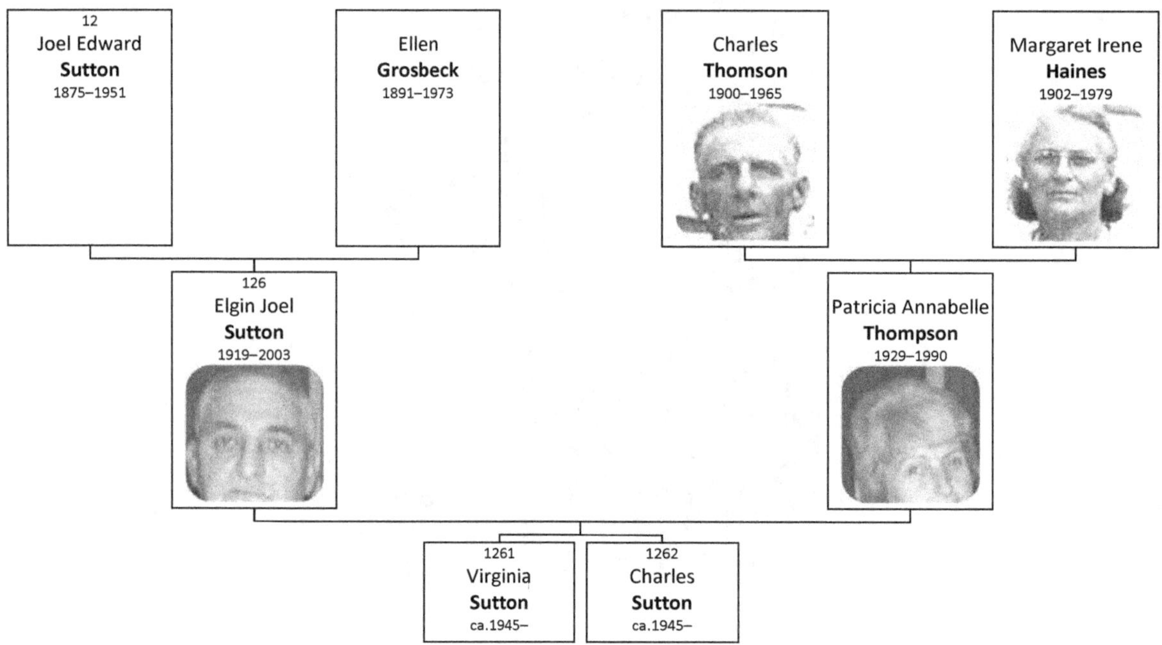

1261. **Virginia**[5] **Sutton** was born about 1945 at (Likely) in London, Middlesex, Ontario, Canada. She is the daughter of Elgin Joel Sutton (126) and Patricia Annabelle Thompson.

Charles Sutton

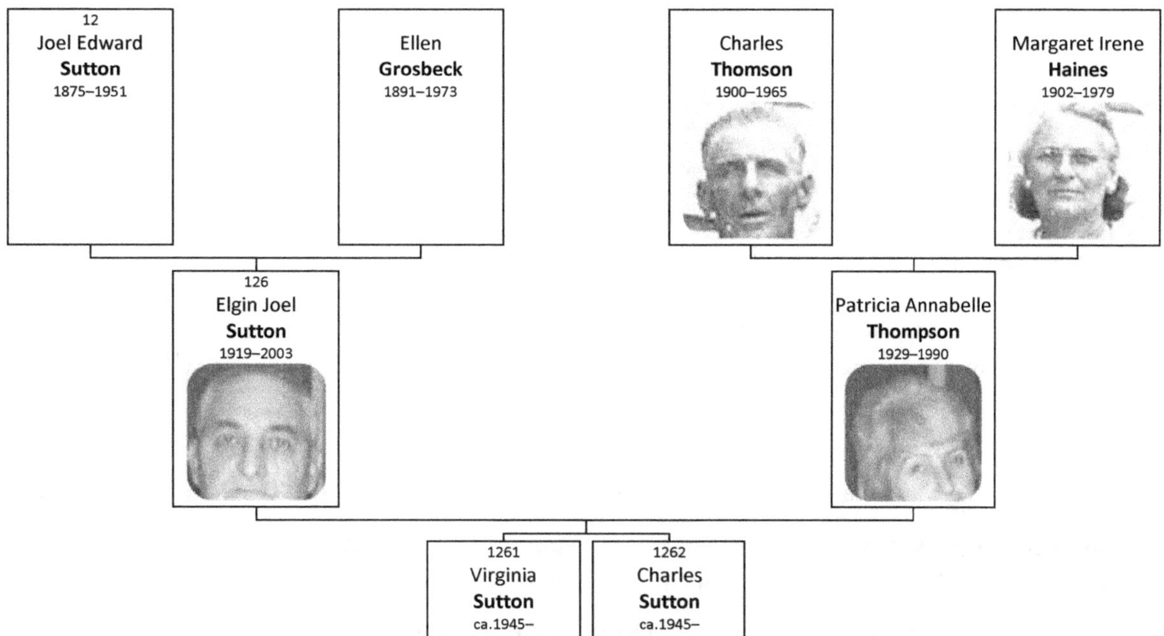

1262. **Charles[5] Sutton** was born about 1945 at (Likely) in London, Middlesex, Ontario, Canada. He is the son of Elgin Joel Sutton (126) and Patricia Annabelle Thompson.

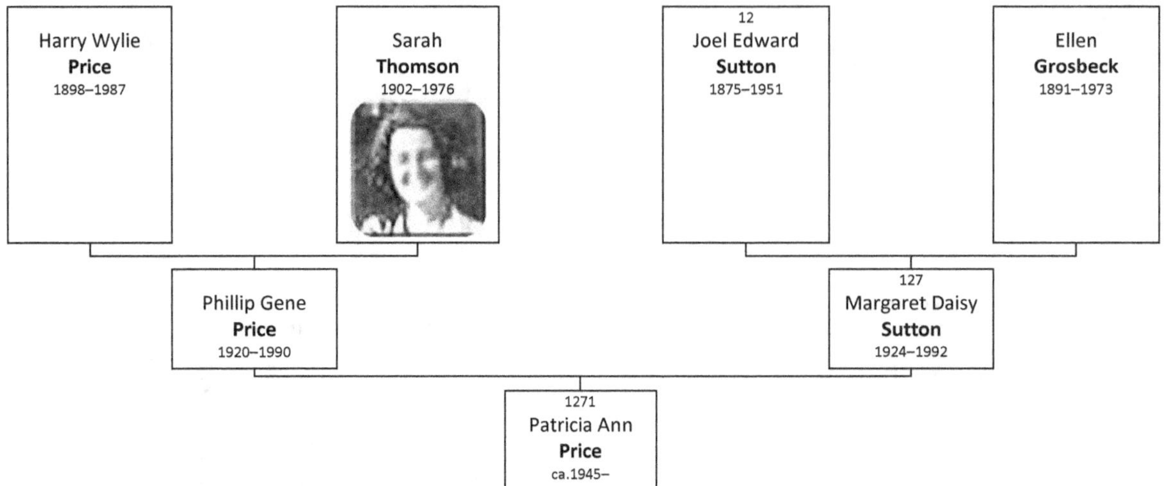

127. **Margaret Daisy[4] Sutton** was born on Monday, September 1, 1924, at Dutton in Elgin, Ontario, Canada.[119–122] She was the daughter of Joel Edward Sutton (12) and Ellen Grosbeck.

Margaret Daisy died in Fort Myers, Lee, Florida, USA, on May 9, 1992, at the age of 67.[119–122]

More facts and events for Margaret Daisy Sutton:

Residence: 1962   London, Middlesex, Ontario, Canada[123]
Cohab: Phillip G   Sutton (Hotel Manager), Mrs Margaret Sutton

Residence: 1968   London, Middlesex, Ontario, Canada[123]
Cohab: Phillip G   Sutton (Hotel Manager), Mrs Margaret Sutton

Residence: 1974   Florida, USA[122]

They had one daughter: Patricia (ca.1945–). Phillip Gene Price was born in Windsor, Essex, Ontario, Canada, on Sunday, December 26, 1920.[124–127] He was the son of Harry Wylie Price and Sarah Thomson.

119   Ancestry.com, U.S., Social Security Applications and Claims Index, 1936-2007 (Provo, UT, USA, Ancestry.com Operations, Inc., 2015), Ancestry.com.

120   Ancestry.com, Beta: Newspapers.com Obituary Index, 1940-1955 (Lehi, UT, USA, Ancestry.com Operations Inc, 2019), Ancestry.com, News-Press; Publication Date: 11/ May/ 1992; Publication Place: Fort Myers, Florida, United States of America; URL: https://www.newspapers.com/image/217181316/?article=aac2d0e3-48a0-4dda-b8ff-ee9caa41eb71&focus=0.19546549,0.75934625,0.354052 16,0.82242817&x.

121   Ancestry.com, Florida Death Index, 1877-1998 (Provo, UT, USA, Ancestry.com Operations Inc, 2004), Ancestry.com.

122   Ancestry.com, U.S., Social Security Death Index, 1935-Current (Provo, UT, USA, Ancestry.com Operations Inc, 2011), Ancestry.com, Social Security Administration; Washington D.C., USA; Social Security Death Index, Master File.

123   Ancestry.com, Canada, Voters Lists, 1935-1980 (Provo, UT, USA, Ancestry.com Operations, Inc., 2012), Ancestry.com, Library and Archives Canada; Ottawa, Ontario, Canada; Voters Lists, Federal Elections, 1935-1980.
[Source citation includes one media item]

124   Ancestry.com, Web: Canada, GenWeb Cemetery Index (Provo, UT, USA, Ancestry.com Operations, Inc., 2013), Ancestry.com.

125   Ancestry.com and Genealogical Research Library (Brampton, Ontario, Canada), Ontario, Canada, Marriages, 1801-1928 (Provo, UT, USA, Ancestry.com Operations, Inc., 2010), Ancestry.com, Archives of Ontario; Archives of Ontario; Registrations of Marriages; Reel: 12-333.
[Source citation includes one media item]

126   Ancestry.com, 1921 Census of Canada (Provo, UT, USA, Ancestry.com Operations Inc, 2013), Ancestry.com, Reference Number: RG 31; Folder Number: 57; Census Place: 57, Essex North, Ontario; Page Number: 5.
[Source citation includes one media item]

Phillip Gene reached 69 years of age and died at (Likely) in London, Middlesex, Ontario, Canada, in 1990.[124] He was buried in London, Middlesex, Ontario, Canada.[124]

More facts and events for Phillip Gene Price:

Residence: June 1, 1921   Windsor, Essex, Ontario, Canada[126]
Residence Religion: Single;   Son / Cohab: Harry Price 23,   Sarah Price 19, Philip Price 5/12,   Sidny Pemprase 30.

Residence: 1949   Elgin, Ontario, Canada[123]
Cohab: Harry Price (Farmer), Mrs Sarah Price, Phillip Price (farmer)

Residence: 1962   London, Middlesex, Ontario, Canada[123]
Cohab: Phillip G   Sutton (Hotel Manager), Mrs Margaret Sutton

Residence: 1968   London, Middlesex, Ontario, Canada[123]
Cohab: Phillip G   Sutton (Hotel Manager), Mrs Margaret Sutton

---

127   Ancestry.com, Detroit Border Crossings and Passenger and Crew Lists, 1905-1957 (Provo, UT, USA, Ancestry.com Operations Inc, 2006), Ancestry.com, The National Archives at Washington, D.C; Washington, D.C.; Series Title: Card Manifests (Alphabetical) of Individuals Entering through the Port of Detroit, Michigan, 1906-1954; NAI: 4527226; Record Group Title: Records of the Immigration and Naturalizatio. [Source citation includes one media item]

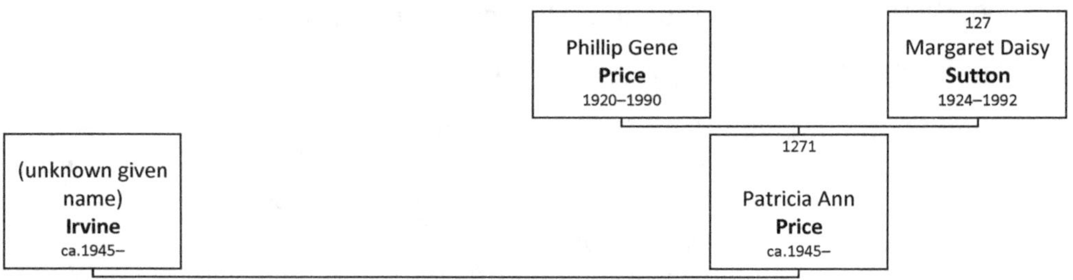

1271. **Patricia Ann^5 Price** was born about 1945 at (Likely), Dutton in Elgin, Ontario, Canada. She is the daughter of Phillip Gene Price and Margaret Daisy Sutton (127).

(unknown given name) Irvine was born at (Likely) in Middlesex, Ontario, Canada, about 1945.

Carman Sutton

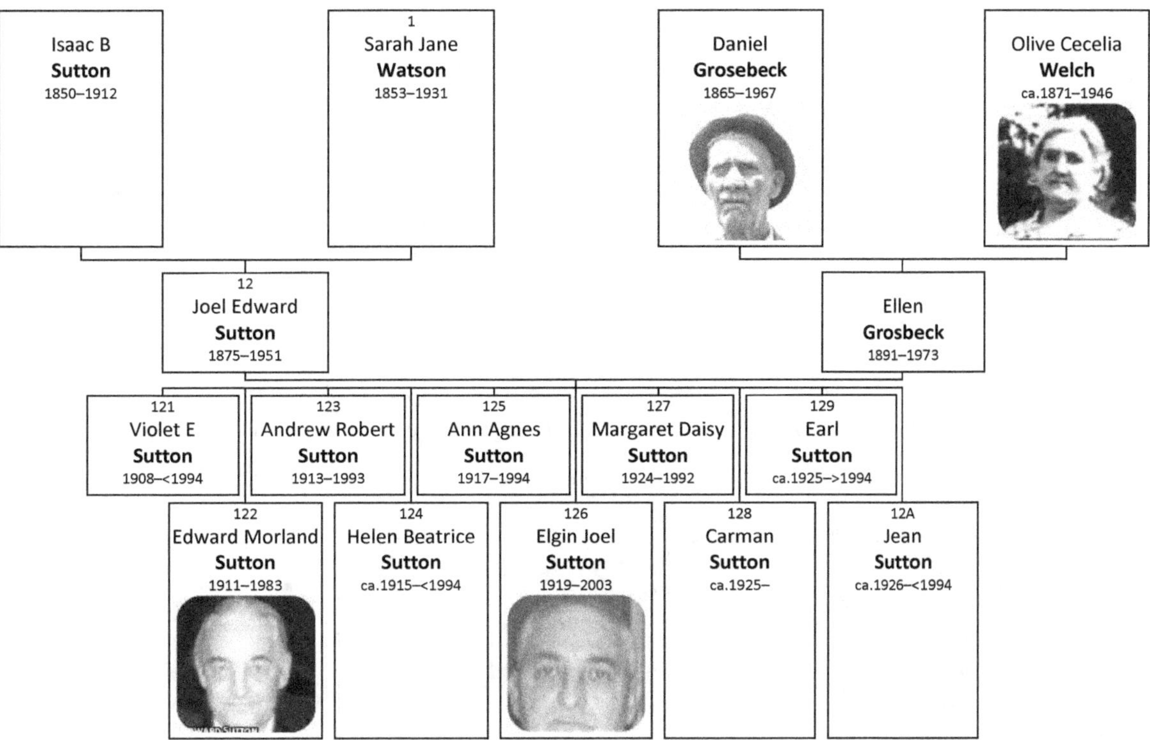

128. **Carman**[4] **Sutton** was born about 1925 at (Likely) in Elgin, Ontario, Canada. He is the son of Joel Edward Sutton (12) and Ellen Grosbeck.

More facts and events for Carman Sutton:

Residence: 1953 Elgin, Ontario, Canada[128]
Cohab: Carman Sutton (Labourer)

Residence: 1965 Elgin, Ontario, Canada[128]
Cohab: Carman Sutton (labourer); Mrs Carman Sutton

Residence: 1968 Elgin, Ontario, Canada[128]
Cohab: Carman Sutton (labourer); Mrs Carman Sutton

Residence: 1972 Elgin, Ontario, Canada[128]
Cohab: Carman Sutton (welder); Mrs Carman Sutton

Residence: 1974 Elgin, Ontario, Canada[128]
Cohab: Carman Sutton (Union Gas); Mrs Carman Sutton (housewife)

---

128 Ancestry.com, Canada, Voters Lists, 1935-1980 (Provo, UT, USA, Ancestry.com Operations, Inc., 2012), Ancestry.com, Library and Archives Canada; Ottawa, Ontario, Canada; Voters Lists, Federal Elections, 1935-1980.
[Source citation includes one media item]

Earl Sutton

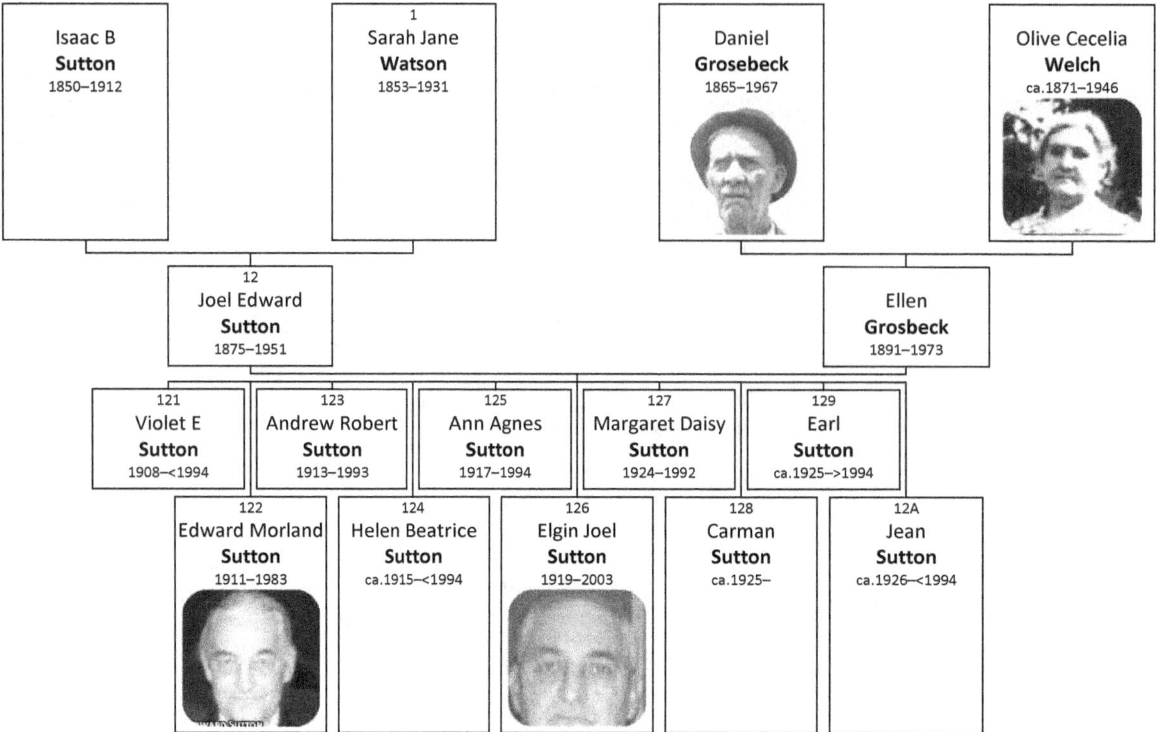

129. **Earl**[4] **Sutton** was born about 1925 at (Likely) in Elgin, Ontario, Canada. He was the son of Joel Edward Sutton (12) and Ellen Grosbeck.

Earl died after 1994.

More facts and events for Earl Sutton:

Residence:	1968	St Thomas, Elgin, Ontario, Canada[129]
		Cohab: Earl Sutton (labourer); Ellen Sutton (Widow)
Residence:	1972	St Thomas, Elgin, Ontario, Canada[129]
		Cohab: Earl Sutton (unemployed); Ellen Sutton
Residence:	1974	St Thomas, Elgin, Ontario, Canada[129]
		Cohab: Earl Sutton (labourer)
Residence:	April 11, 1994	Elgin, Ontario, Canada
		Residence cited in mother's obituary.

129 Ancestry.com, Canada, Voters Lists, 1935-1980 (Provo, UT, USA, Ancestry.com Operations, Inc., 2012), Ancestry.com, Library and Archives Canada; Ottawa, Ontario, Canada; Voters Lists, Federal Elections, 1935-1980.
[Source citation includes one media item]

Family of Jean Sutton and Atkinson

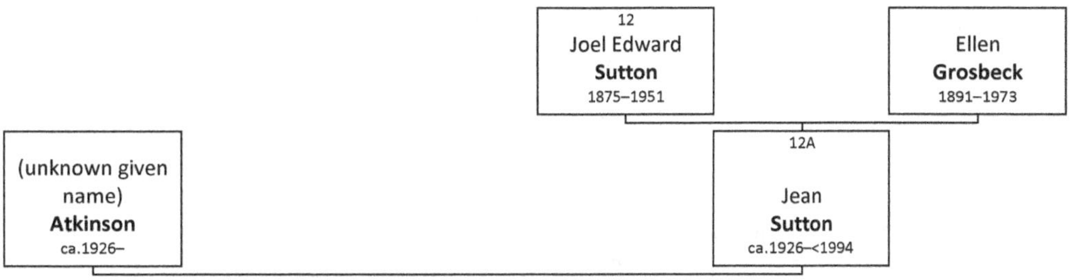

12A. **Jean**[4] **Sutton** was born about 1926 at (Likely) in Elgin, Ontario, Canada. She was the daughter of Joel Edward Sutton (12) and Ellen Grosbeck.

Jean died before 1994. Mentioned as deceased in mother's obituary.

(unknown given name) Atkinson was born at (Likely) in Elgin, Ontario, Canada, about 1926.

Ann Sutton

13.   **Ann A[3] Sutton** was born on Monday, June 3, 1878, at Dutton in Elgin, Ontario, Canada.[130–137] She was the daughter of Isaac B Sutton and Sarah Jane Watson (1).

Ann A died in Kern, California, USA, on December 18, 1973, at the age of 95.[135, 136]

More facts and events for Ann A Sutton:

Residence: 1891   Elgin, Ontario, Canada[131]
Single;   Dau / Cohab: Isaac Sutton 41,   Janes Sutton 37,   Andrew Sutton 18,   Joe Sutton 16,   Annie Sutton 12.

Residence: 1901   Elgin, Ontario, Canada[130]
Married; : Dau / Cohab: Isac Sutton 57,   Sarah J Sutton 47,   Joel Sutton 26,   Annie McGill 22.

Residence: 1920   Kern, California, USA[133]
Married;   Wife / Cohab: Robert W Mcgill 43,   Anna C Mcgill 40,   George B Mcgill 16, Harry Vorhees 40,   George O Strickland 20,   Avard Swanson 50,   John H Werley 56, James N Vorhees 46,   Edson Archibald 24.

Residence: 1926   Bakersfield, Kern, California, USA[138]

Residence: 1927   Bakersfield, Kern, California, USA[138]

Residence: 1930   Bakersfield, Kern, California, USA[134]
Married;   Wife / Cohab: Wesley R Mcgill 53,   Annie L Mcgill 51,   George B Mcgill 24, Sarah J Sutton 77.

Residence: 1931   Bakersfield, Kern, California, USA[138]

Residence: 1935   Bakersfield, Kern, California, USA[137]

Residence: 1940   Bakersfield, Kern, California, USA[137]
Widowed; Head; Owner-Manager of Annie McGill Dairy / Cohab: Annie McGill 59

Residence: 1962   California, USA[136]

[130] Ancestry.com, 1901 Census of Canada (Provo, UT, USA, Ancestry.com Operations Inc, 2006), Ancestry.com, Year: 1901; Census Place: Dutton (Village), Elgin (west/ouest), Ontario; Page: 15; Family No: 175.
[Source citation includes one media item]

[131] Ancestry.com, 1891 Census of Canada (Provo, UT, USA, Ancestry.com Operations Inc, 2008), Ancestry.com, Year: 1891; Census Place: Dunwich, Elgin West, Ontario; Roll: T-6334; Family No: 57.
[Source citation includes one media item]

[132] Ancestry.com and Genealogical Research Library (Brampton, Ontario, Canada), Ontario, Canada, Marriages, 1801-1928 (Provo, UT, USA, Ancestry.com Operations, Inc., 2010), Ancestry.com, Archives of Ontario; Toronto, Ontario, Canada; Registrations of Marriages, 1869-1928; Series: MS932; Reel: 100.
[Source citation includes one media item]

[133] Ancestry.com, 1920 United States Federal Census (Provo, UT, USA, Ancestry.com Operations Inc, 2010), Ancestry.com, Year: 1920; Census Place: Township 15, Kern, California; Roll: T625_100; Page: 24B; Enumeration District: 110; Image: 880.
[Source citation includes one media item]

[134] Ancestry.com, 1930 United States Federal Census (Provo, UT, USA, Ancestry.com Operations Inc, 2002), Ancestry.com, Year: 1930; Census Place: Bakersfield, Kern, California; Roll: 121; Page: 2A; Enumeration District: 0016; Image: 881.0; FHL microfilm: 2339856.
[Source citation includes one media item]

[135] Ancestry.com, California, Death Index, 1940-1997 (Provo, UT, USA, Ancestry.com Operations Inc, 2000), Ancestry.com, Date: 1973-12-18.

[136] Ancestry.com, U.S., Social Security Death Index, 1935-Current (Provo, UT, USA, Ancestry.com Operations Inc, 2011), Ancestry.com, Social Security Administration; Washington D.C., USA; Social Security Death Index, Master File.

[137] Ancestry.com, 1940 United States Federal Census (Provo, UT, USA, Ancestry.com Operations, Inc., 2012), Ancestry.com, Year: 1940; Census Place: Bakersfield, Kern, California; Roll: m-t0627-00212; Page: 61A; Enumeration District: 15-25.
[Source citation includes one media item]

[138] Ancestry.com, U.S. City Directories, 1821-1989 (Provo, UT, USA, Ancestry.com Operations, Inc., 2011), Ancestry.com.
[Source citation includes one media item]

Marriages with Robert Wesley McGill and an unknown partner are known.

Family of Ann Sutton and Robert McGill

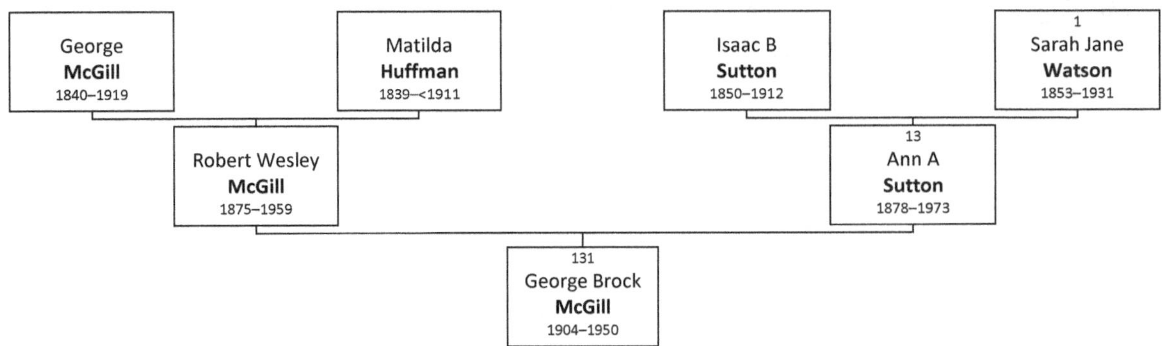

Here are the details about **Ann A Sutton's** first marriage with Robert Wesley McGill. You can read more about Ann A on page 72.

They had one son: George (1904–1950). Robert Wesley McGill was born in Petrolia, Lambton, Ontario, Canada, on Saturday, December 11, 1875.[132–134, 139–143] He was the son of George McGill and Matilda Huffman.

Robert Wesley reached 83 years of age and died at (Likely) in Bakersfield, Kern, California, USA, in 1959.[144]

More facts and events for Robert Wesley McGill:

Residence: 1881 Petrolia, Lambton, Ontario, Canada[141]
Cohab: George McGill 40, Matilda McGill 41, George Colin McGill 13, Flora Hester McGill 11, King McGill 9, Herbert McGill 7, Robert Wesley McGill 5, Mary Margaret McGill 3/12, George Stenson 20.

Residence: 1891 Petrolia, Lambton, Ontario, Canada[142]
Single; Son / Cohab: George McGill 50, Matelda Huffman 51, Colin McGill 23, Flora McGill 21, Renz McGill 19, Habert McGill 17, ??Sley McGill 15, Margaret McGill 10.

Residence: 1901 Toronto, Ontario, Canada[143]
Married; S-in-L; Bookbinder / Cohab: Henry Ebersfield 61, Eleanor Ebersfield 53, Annie McGill 28, William Ebersfield 25, Robt McGill 25.

139   Ancestry.com, Ontario, Canada Births, 1869-1913 (Provo, UT, USA, Ancestry.com Operations Inc, 2010), Ancestry.com, Archives of Ontario; Series: MS929; Reel: 23.
[Source citation includes one media item]

140   Ancestry.com, U.S., World War I Draft Registration Cards, 1917-1918 (Provo, UT, USA, Ancestry.com Operations Inc, 2005), Ancestry.com, Registration State: California; Registration County: Kern; Roll: 1530796; Draft Board: 2.
[Source citation includes one media item]

141   Ancestry.com and The Church of Jesus Christ of Latter-day Saints, 1881 Census of Canada (Provo, UT, USA, Ancestry.com Operations Inc, 2009), Ancestry.com, Year: 1881; Census Place: Petrolia, Lambton, Ontario; Roll: C_13277; Page: 13; Family No: 56.
[Source citation includes one media item]

142   Ancestry.com, 1891 Census of Canada (Provo, UT, USA, Ancestry.com Operations Inc, 2008), Ancestry.com, Year: 1891; Census Place: Petrolia, Lambton East, Ontario; Roll: T-6347; Family No: 1.
[Source citation includes one media item]

143   Ancestry.com, 1901 Census of Canada (Provo, UT, USA, Ancestry.com Operations Inc, 2006), Ancestry.com, Year: 1901; Census Place: Toronto (City/Cité) Ward/Quartier No 3, York (East/est), Ontario; Page: 13; Family No: 131.
[Source citation includes one media item]

144   Ancestry.com, Ohio Obituary Index, 1830s-2011, Rutherford B. Hayes Presidential Center (Provo, UT, USA, Ancestry.com Operations, Inc., 2010), Ancestry.com, Rutherford B. Hayes Presidential Center; Spiegel Grove, Fremont, Ohio; Rutherford B. Hayes Presidential Center Ohio Obituary Index, 1830s to 2011.

Residence: 1920   Kern, California, USA[133]

Married; Widow;   Head; Superintendent Tannehill Oil Company / Cohab: Robert W Mcgill 43,   Anna C Mcgill 40,   George B Mcgill 16,   Harry Vorhees 40,   George O Strickland 20,   Avard Swanson 50,   John H Werley 56,   James N Vorhees 46,   Edson Archibald 24.

Residence: 1926   Bakersfield, Kern, California, USA[138]

Residence: 1927   Bakersfield, Kern, California, USA[138]

Residence: 1930   Bakersfield, Kern, California, USA[134]

Married;   Head / Cohab: Wesley R Mcgill 53,   Annie L Mcgill 51,   George B Mcgill 24, Sarah J Sutton 77.

Residence: 1931   Bakersfield, Kern, California, USA[138]

George McGill

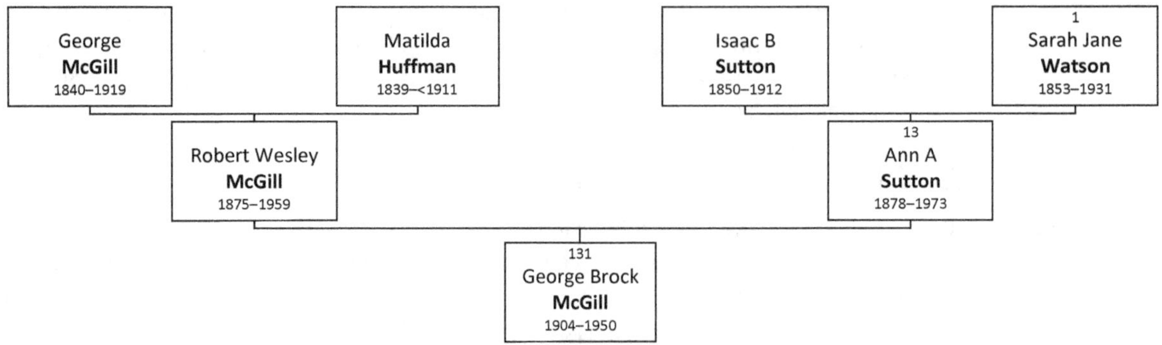

131. **George Brock**[4] **McGill** was born on Tuesday, November 8, 1904, in Bakersfield, Kern, California, USA.[145–149] He was the son of Robert Wesley McGill and Ann A Sutton (13).

George Brock died in Kern, California, USA, on May 20, 1950, at the age of 45.[147]

More facts and events for George Brock McGill:

Residence: June 30, 1913   California, USA[149]
Relation to Head of House: Son

Residence: 1920   Kern, California, USA[145]
Single;   Son   / Cohab: Robert W Mcgill 43,   Anna C Mcgill 40,   George B Mcgill 16,   Harry Vorhees 40,   George O Strickland 20,   Avard Swanson 50, John H Werley 56,   James N Vorhees 46,   Edson Archibald 24.

Residence: 1924 - 1932   Kern, California, USA[150]
Party Affiliation: Republican,   Occupation: Oil Worker

Residence: 1925   Bakersfield, Kern, California, USA[151]
Occupation: Oilwkr

Residence: 1930   Bakersfield, Kern, California, USA[146]
Single; Son / Cohab: Wesley R Mcgill 53,   Annie L Mcgill 51,   George B Mcgill 24,   Sarah J Sutton 77.

Residence: 1940   Kern, California, USA[148]

---

145   Ancestry.com, 1920 United States Federal Census (Provo, UT, USA, Ancestry.com Operations Inc, 2010), Ancestry.com, Year: 1920; Census Place: Township 15, Kern, California; Roll: T625_100; Page: 24B; Enumeration District: 110; Image: 880.
[Source citation includes one media item]

146   Ancestry.com, 1930 United States Federal Census (Provo, UT, USA, Ancestry.com Operations Inc, 2002), Ancestry.com, Year: 1930; Census Place: Bakersfield, Kern, California; Roll: 121; Page: 2A; Enumeration District: 0016; Image: 881.0; FHL microfilm: 2339856.
[Source citation includes one media item]

147   Ancestry.com, California, Death Index, 1940-1997 (Provo, UT, USA, Ancestry.com Operations Inc, 2000), Ancestry.com, Date: 1950-05-20.

148   Ancestry.com, U.S. WWII Draft Cards Young Men, 1940-1947 (Provo, UT, USA, Ancestry.com Operations, Inc., 2011), Ancestry.com, The National Archives in St. Louis, Missouri; St. Louis, Missouri; WWII Draft Registration Cards for California, 10/16/1940-03/31/1947; Record Group: Records of the Selective Service System, 147; Box: 1176.
[Source citation includes one media item]

149   Ancestry.com, U.S., Indian Census Rolls, 1885-1940 (Provo, UT, USA, Ancestry.com Operations Inc, 2007), Ancestry.com, Year: 1913; Roll: M595_13; Line: 23; Agency: Soboba.
[Source citation includes one media item]

150   Ancestry.com, California, Voter Registrations, 1900-1968 (Provo, UT, USA, Ancestry.com Operations Inc, 2017), Ancestry.com, California State Library; Sacramento, California; Great Register of Voters, 1900-1968.
[Source citation includes one media item]

151   Ancestry.com, U.S. City Directories, 1821-1989 (Provo, UT, USA, Ancestry.com Operations, Inc., 2011), Ancestry.com.
[Source citation includes one media item]

Employer: Annie Mcgill Dairy,   Weight: 185,   Complexion: Dark,   Eye Color: Hazel,   Hair Color: Brown,   Height: 5 10.

Ann Sutton

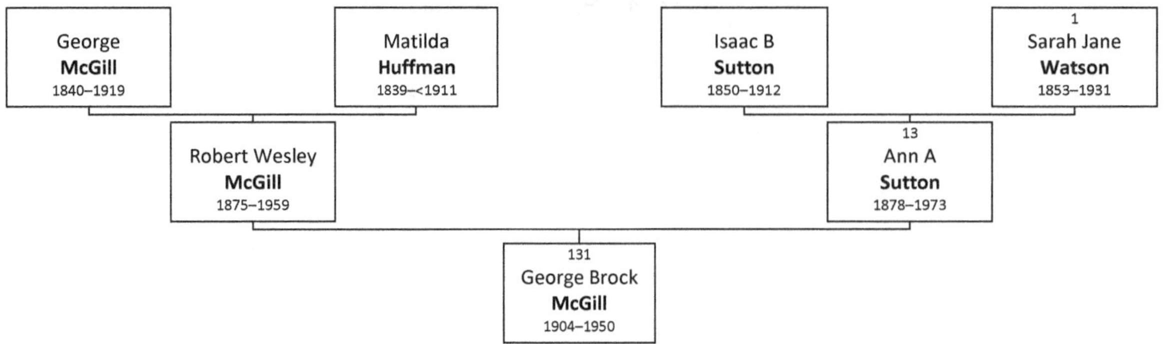

Here are the details about **Ann A Sutton's** second marriage with an unknown partner. You can read more about Ann A on page 72.

Bibliography

Ancestry.com and Genealogical Research Library (Brampton, Ontario, Canada). *Ontario, Canada, Marriages, 1801-1928*. Provo, UT, USA: Ancestry.com Operations, Inc., 2010.

Ancestry.com and The Church of Jesus Christ of Latter-day Saints. *1861 Census of Canada*. Provo, UT, USA: Ancestry.com Operations Inc, 2009.

Ancestry.com and The Church of Jesus Christ of Latter-day Saints. *1871 Census of Canada*. Provo, UT, USA: Ancestry.com Operations Inc, 2009.

Ancestry.com and The Church of Jesus Christ of Latter-day Saints. *1881 Census of Canada*. Provo, UT, USA: Ancestry.com Operations Inc, 2009.

Ancestry.com and The Church of Jesus Christ of Latter-day Saints. *1916 Canada Census of Manitoba, Saskatchewan, and Alberta*. Provo, UT, USA: Ancestry.com Operations Inc, 2009.

Ancestry.com. *1851 Census of Canada East, Canada West, New Brunswick, and Nova Scotia*. Provo, UT, USA: Ancestry.com Operations Inc, 2006.

Ancestry.com. *1891 Census of Canada*. Provo, UT, USA: Ancestry.com Operations Inc, 2008.

Ancestry.com. *1901 Census of Canada*. Provo, UT, USA: Ancestry.com Operations Inc, 2006.

Ancestry.com. *1906 Canada Census of Manitoba, Saskatchewan, and Alberta*. Provo, UT, USA: Ancestry.com Operations Inc, 2006.

Ancestry.com. *1911 Census of Canada*. Provo, UT, USA: Ancestry.com Operations Inc, 2006.

Ancestry.com. *1920 United States Federal Census*. Provo, UT, USA: Ancestry.com Operations Inc, 2010.

Ancestry.com. *1921 Census of Canada*. Provo, UT, USA: Ancestry.com Operations Inc, 2013.

Ancestry.com. *1930 United States Federal Census*. Provo, UT, USA: Ancestry.com Operations Inc, 2002.

Ancestry.com. *1940 United States Federal Census*. Provo, UT, USA: Ancestry.com Operations, Inc., 2012.

Ancestry.com. *Beta: Newspapers.com Obituary Index, 1940-1955*. Lehi, UT, USA: Ancestry.com Operations Inc, 2019.

Ancestry.com. *California, Death Index, 1905-1939*. Provo, UT, USA: Ancestry.com Operations, Inc., 2013.

Ancestry.com. *California, Death Index, 1940-1997*. Provo, UT, USA: Ancestry.com Operations Inc, 2000.

Ancestry.com. *California, Voter Registrations, 1900-1968*. Provo, UT, USA: Ancestry.com Operations Inc, 2017.

Ancestry.com. *Canada Obituary Collection*. Provo, UT, USA: Ancestry.com Operations Inc, 2006.

Ancestry.com. *Canada, Find A Grave Index, 1600s-Current*. Provo, UT, USA: Ancestry.com Operations, Inc., 2012.

Ancestry.com. *Canada, Selected School Yearbooks, 1908-2010*. Provo, UT, USA: Ancestry.com Operations, Inc., 2015.

Ancestry.com. *Canada, Soldiers of the First World War, 1914-1918*. Provo, UT, USA: Ancestry.com Operations, Inc., 2006.

Ancestry.com. *Canada, Voters Lists, 1935-1980*. Provo, UT, USA: Ancestry.com Operations, Inc., 2012.

Ancestry.com. *Canada, WWI CEF Personnel Files, 1914-1918*. Lehi, UT, USA: Ancestry.com Operations, Inc., 2016.

Ancestry.com. *Canadian Phone and Address Directories, 1995-2002*. Provo, UT, USA: Ancestry.com Operations Inc, 2005.

Ancestry.com. *Detroit Border Crossings and Passenger and Crew Lists, 1905-1957*. Provo, UT, USA: Ancestry.com Operations Inc, 2006.

Ancestry.com. *Florida Death Index, 1877-1998*. Provo, UT, USA: Ancestry.com Operations Inc, 2004.

Ancestry.com. *Ohio Obituary Index, 1830s-2011, Rutherford B. Hayes Presidential Center*. Provo, UT, USA: Ancestry.com Operations, Inc., 2010.

Ancestry.com. *Ontario, Canada Births, 1869-1913*. Provo, UT, USA: Ancestry.com Operations Inc, 2010.

Ancestry.com. *Ontario, Canada, Deaths, 1869-1938 and Deaths Overseas, 1939-1947*. Provo, UT, USA: Ancestry.com Operations Inc, 2010.

Ancestry.com. *Oregon, Death Index, 1898-2008*. Provo, UT, USA: Ancestry.com Operations Inc, 2000.

Ancestry.com. *U.S. Cemetery and Funeral Home Collection*. Provo, UT, USA: Ancestry.com Operations Inc, 2011.

Ancestry.com. *U.S. City Directories, 1821-1989*. Provo, UT, USA: Ancestry.com Operations, Inc., 2011.

Ancestry.com. *U.S. Public Records Index, Volume 2*. Provo, UT, USA: Ancestry.com Operations, Inc., 2010.

Ancestry.com. *U.S. World War II Navy Muster Rolls, 1938-1949*. Provo, UT, USA: Ancestry.com Operations Inc, 2011.

Ancestry.com. *U.S. WWII Draft Cards Young Men, 1940-1947*. Provo, UT, USA: Ancestry.com Operations, Inc., 2011.

Ancestry.com. *U.S., Find A Grave Index, 1700s-Current*. Provo, UT, USA: Ancestry.com Operations, Inc., 2012.

Ancestry.com. *U.S., Indian Census Rolls, 1885-1940*. Provo, UT, USA: Ancestry.com Operations Inc, 2007.

Ancestry.com. *U.S., Railroad Retirement Pension Index, 1934-1987*. Lehi, UT, USA: Ancestry.com Operations, Inc., 2017.

Ancestry.com. *U.S., Social Security Applications and Claims Index, 1936-2007*. Provo, UT, USA: Ancestry.com Operations, Inc., 2015.

Ancestry.com. *U.S., Social Security Death Index, 1935-Current*. Provo, UT, USA: Ancestry.com Operations Inc, 2011.

Ancestry.com. *U.S., World War I Draft Registration Cards, 1917-1918*. Provo, UT, USA: Ancestry.com Operations Inc, 2005.

Ancestry.com. *UK, Allied Prisoners of War, 1939-1945*. Lehi, UT, USA: Ancestry.com Operations, Inc., 2018.

Ancestry.com. *Web: Canada, GenWeb Cemetery Index*. Provo, UT, USA: Ancestry.com Operations, Inc., 2013.

Ancestry.com. *Web: Manitoba, Birth Index, 1866-1912*. Provo, UT, USA: Ancestry.com Operations, Inc., 2013.

Ancestry.com. *Web: Manitoba, Death Index, 1881-1941*. Provo, UT, USA: Ancestry.com Operations, Inc., 2012.

Ancestry.com. *Web: Obituary Daily Times Index, 1995-2012*. Provo, UT, USA: Ancestry.com Operations, Inc., 2012.

Index of Places

Index of Individuals

www.ingramcontent.com/pod-product-compliance
Lightning Source LLC
Chambersburg PA
CBHW081735250726
48657CB00010B/3275